T0208230

Glimpse
A Telling Tattle

D.S.
Sully

iUniverse, Inc.
Bloomington

Glimpse
A Telling Tattle

iUniverse books may be ordered through booksellers or by contacting:

iUniverse
1663 Liberty Drive
Bloomington, IN 47403
www.iuniverse.com
1-800-Authors (1-800-288-4677)

ISBN: 978-1-4620-0032-6 (sc)
ISBN: 978-1-4620-0033-3 (ebook)

Printed in the United States of America

iUniverse rev. date: 03/23/2011

Contents

Acknowledgments

This book is dedicated to Dianna, who has endured far too many of the shenanigans encompassed in these stories. It is also dedicated to my mother, Esther, whose lifelong battle with arthritis taught me all about adversity and how to weather just about any storm.

Reference note: All quotes featured at the beginning of each chapter are those of the author.

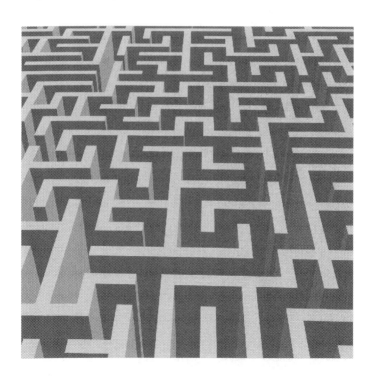

Perhaps if you act owlishly enough and give a hoot, you may eventually become a wise old bird.

Introduction

Nobody's perfect, yet each of us strive to fit in by ignoring, avoiding, or battling the imperfections. Should challenges arise in doing so, you then *"fit out"* by *outlasting* the doubters, *outshining* the dark moments, and *outmaneuvering* the obstacles, none of which comes easy. This I know because of the lessons taught to me by a real life Santa, a gun-toting mobster, a wooly mammoth of a street musician, a gothic grade school teacher, a revealing campus streaker, a Bataan Death March survivor, a hobbit on skis, a handy guardian angel, a genuine Beetle Bailey, a crotchety old wrangler, and some persevering Vietnam veterans.

Writing this book might be the hardest thing I've ever done. It is a tattled tale of caricatures and conundrums. Many sleepless nights resulted while contemplating these stories. Perhaps this is caused by never being altogether comfortable with the main character, which, by the way, happens to be me.

At first, I wanted to sugar-coat everything and only emphasize the comical episodes of my life. However, that would not be right. There has been a contrast between incredibly good and despicably bad times, all needing to be equally noted. Sharing all the details does not come easy. It never has and never will. This is due to the reality of living in a world that differs from most others. It also stems from being relegated to a role that is indeed complicated, confusing, and oftentimes isolating. And even though this leads me to consider myself a misfit minority, it's quite possible that some will disagree.

What will now be endeavored is a glimpse from the eyes of the beholder. It is a view into the only world known to me. Along with the comedies, there have been sad-sack events and gut-wrenching moments, many of which will now resurface as unique and outlandish.

Let me put all this into perspective by explaining that slowly but surely, I am losing my senses. To be meticulously precise, it is one sense in particular. As such, I find myself defiantly crossing over to the dark side. Though resistance may seem futile, pursuing a light at the end of the tunnel is a continuing challenge that more than meets the eye. While doing so, I've acquainted myself with some interesting characters, established close ties, encountered far too many predicaments, and grew up learning from four British lads named John, Paul, George, and Ringo, who advised me to get by "With a Little Help from My Friends."

Thus what you are about to get a glimpse of is a haphazard sojourn through far too many quandaries. Therefore, abandon any farfetched notions of an enchanted fairytale and prepare for a bantered saga of brandished revelations. While some may inspire and others raise ire, each one is wholeheartedly presented, just the way I see it.

Wuthering Frights

Being unique is something we all have in common. Adapting to this uniqueness is what differentiates each of us.

J ust three months into third grade, I experienced the scariest moment of my young life. Occurring in late autumn of 1963, this harrowing episode had nothing to do with a war in Vietnam, civil rights protests, Russian missiles, or even the horrifying assassination of a beloved president. All these were beyond my fledgling comprehension. Instead, foremost to me at this time was contending with the formidable Ms. Alice and the parochial discipline of St. Joseph's Catholic School. This truly mattered, for what I was about to commit seemed like a mortal sin.

First and second grades were pretty much a breeze. Led by smiling young nuns in long black robes and high-rise headgear, these tranquil settings, left little to fear. This serenity was about to change, however, due to a third grade drill sergeant, who religiously mustered her class into rigorous academic readiness.

Known at St. Joe's for her divine intervention of knuckle–whacking, ear pulling, and intimidating body language, Ms. Alice was an elementary force to be reckoned with. Her demeanor of true grit and gruff commands, contrasted with an endearing grandmotherly veneer that fooled no one. Beneath silvery hair and behind her wire-rimmed glasses, a piercing glare often sent shivers down one's spine. The seismic crack, which rippled from top to bottom of the front blackboard, served as a legendary memorial to even tougher tactics by this far-from-mild-mannered mentor. The long wooden pointer, routinely clutched in Ms. Alice's right hand, became an educational tool for stinging lessons. Not to be ignored as well was the corner supply closet, which, when necessary, quickly transformed into a makeshift juvenile detention cell. And of course, filling the entire blackboard with repetitious sentences served as her standard after-school penance for misbehavior. Unbeknownst to me, I would soon be in jeopardy of all these unholy measures. What exactly happened and why is still a haunting mystery to me.

As midday recess ended, my classmates and I reassembled for afternoon music instruction. Ms. Alice immediately began instituting her classroom regiment of holding up flash cards with music symbols and demanding that each student take a turn at identifying them. Being well-versed in the subject matter, I often looked forward to this particular drill. There was no reason for concern when it finally came my turn to recognize the card being held by Ms. Alice. At first there was an eerie silence as I failed to respond. This stalemate quickly ended as Ms. Alice impatiently repeated my name and her command to identify the music symbol. In this era of parochial discipline, any hint of disobedience was both sinful and unacceptable. The dreaded possibility of a knuckle whack or closet confinement now loomed eminently. After hesitating some more, I then answered, "I don't know." Reacting to what she may have comprehended as a forbidden breach of Catholicism, Ms. Alice hesitated as well, expressed a customary glare, and sternly responded, "What do you mean you don't know?" Nervous and befuddled, I had to finally fess up and proclaim, "I can't see the card." As Ms. Alice moved closer and closer, I sensed the stares of the entire classroom. At last, she got within redemptive range for me to blurt out, "It's a treble clef." As the right answer in a wrong situation, this meant trouble and I was scared silly. Would I now suffer the wrath of Ms. Alice or face the equally frightening consequence of being sent for consultation with Father John?

Hunched forward in my pint-sized desk and staring

downward, I felt alone and terrified. An air of uncertainty now surrounded me. As a young pup haplessly relegated to the foreboding doghouse, I was clueless about how to deal with this adult-sized dilemma. Unfortunately, my teachers, family, friends, and the medical community lacked any concrete solutions as well. Corrective lenses got ruled out immediately by the local optometrist. Freak-out mode became the norm. Guidance counseling and special needs education were yet to exist at this level. Even if they had, it's doubtful as to whether anything would have changed. My predicament was beyond even the highfalutin experts. As such, I suddenly became a puzzle with missing pieces and therefore needed desperate reconfiguration. However, not knowing where to turn to or what to do, this calamity thus transformed my altered focus into wuthering frights.

In this parochial setting of mine, I was now at the mercy of whatever prayers the good sisters of St. Joe's could kneel down and perpetrate on my behalf. From this elementary juncture and until eighth grade graduation, my out-of-sight status became the cause of many calloused knees and tightly folded hands. Also resulting would be the whispered remarks varying from sympathetic sorrows to vented sarcasms. Perhaps the spiritual support from these holy nuns might merit the chance or consideration for an evangelical miracle. On the other hand, praise the Lord that even though Father John was more than capable, Catholic exorcisms had ended a long time ago.

After returning home with a note from Ms. Alice, a landslide of questions and concerns began rolling into my life. Soon it became apparent that no one in this small rural community had any remedies for me. Discombobulated by all this, I then found myself seated in the backseat of the family Oldsmobile and headed to the big city of Madison. My destiny was about to meet with an intense optical interrogation by an ophthalmology specialist. Unaware that my sister,

Kathy, had the same problem, she accompanied me on this enlightening trip. In a few years down the line, my younger brother, Tom, would face the same quandary. Following far too many eye drops, inquisitions, and piercing camera lights, the ophthalmologist rendered his dismal diagnosis. Due to something called macular degeneration, the medical moniker of legally blind was branded upon me. As a disorder usually associated with elderly eyes, the medical terminology not only seemed confusing, but it also bugged me considerably. Why was a young twerp like me being labeled with a term that applied to old geezers who could see little or nothing at all? Such a reference certainly did not represent my circumstance. Adding to the anxiety, it was then noted that this rare condition could not be countered by glasses or surgery and would gradually worsen over time. An uplifting prognosis it was not. In years to come, fancier terms like Stargardt's and *Fundus flavi-maculatus* would further describe my situation.

On the report card of life, I had now been given a "D" and left with little hope of raising this grade. From here on, this kid would need all the extra credit he could earn. Following the prospects of what had just been shared with me, I again found myself scared silly. However, being scared silly can translate into fearing what is yet to come and crazy enough to defy it. From my naïve point of view, this ordeal was more of a problem with how others saw me rather than what I visually perceived. How I looked and acted seemed all that mattered in order to fit in. Among fellow classmates, my primary instinct was to be a buddy and not a bystander, a teammate rather than a spectator, and, most of all, more ordinary than eccentric. To be defined by a limitation was something I could not readily accept. Thus, at the ripe old age of eight, ignorance was bliss and defiance even better. Over the years, this became an ongoing strategy, never to be forsaken. Oftentimes, it became a feisty battle cry as well. In crossing over to the dark side, I was not about to go easily.

As a young whippersnapper, my acuity ever so discretely began matching that of an aging elder. This rare condition at such an early stage, ultimately robs you of your central vision. Sinister and clandestine, the thievery continues slowly but surely. Adhering to boundaries, the progression generally stays clear of the outer reaches used for peripheral sight. Therefore, you retain the vision used primarily to see movements, shapes, contrasts, and configurations, yet gradually lose the ability to focus on the details when reading, writing, and otherwise. In essence, you catch mainly the headlines while struggling with the accompanying stories. However, these same stories can be experienced in other ways, and therein began my challenge of life in these outer limits.

For the most part, the division between peripheral and central vision goes unnoticed by each of us. Normally they are synchronized to work simultaneously. In partnership, each compensates for the other. What happens then when one suddenly begins to go out of kilter? You adapt by changing the viewpoint.

The result of my trip to the eye doctor left me wondering whether this acclaimed expert really knew what he was talking about. Why couldn't he just fix my eyes, why can't someone just give me glasses, and, for crying out loud, why the *"B"* label, when I can still see the world well enough around me? As time wore on, these would become the same questions constantly peppered on me by far too many, who amazingly turned cynical or suspicious when I did not fit their entrenched stereotypes. Others who believed only in all or nothing extremes confounded over anything in between. Never intending to brag about or bemoan this situation, my intensely private nature even got misconstrued as a masquerade of deception. Those, however, attempting to be complimentary, simply exclaimed, "But you seem so normal."

If any of this seems weird to you, just imagine how confusing it was for a kid of only eight years old. Basically, my eyes were like mirrors, smudged rather than broken. By overlooking the clouded areas and concentrating on the shinier surfaces, these mirrors can still be used. However, this compromised view vastly changes the angle at which you approach life.

By virtue of my teachers, coaches, and a fair share of classmates, I became known as the "kid with bad eyes." It seemed like their only way to explain my situation. This was neither a cherished nor favorable title. However, it was accurate for the most part. As for my own perspective, what I continued to see was an ongoing need to fit in, while avoiding any unsavory labels.

At the third grade level, you are not well-equipped to deal with major life changing situations. There are few experiences to fall back on or situations to compare with at this threshold. Within my rural hometown, I felt marooned on an island absent of role models, confidants, and peers. The only lessons on this subject at my parochial school were the biblical passages about the forlorn blind, cripples, and lepers living as outcasts and awaiting random miracles. Even though I elevated myself to devout altar boy status and owned several rosaries, there was not much faith on my part as to the probability of any heaven-sent turnabout.

My only foresight into the future came from elders. There were times when I met senior citizens with depleted vision, whose eyes were worn-out and ancient. Many appeared frustrated or embarrassed about losing view of the world around them. Frightened by the potential loss of their driver's license and independence, some even refused to acknowledge that a problem existed. None of this favored my vision for the years ahead. Too young to know better, I decided to radically resist the negative outlooks and outcomes. Unbeknownst, this would, time and time again, land me in many a doghouse for what some surprisingly chastised as denial and downright obstinacy.

This modest hometown of mine numbered less than four thousand residents. Therefore, you knew everyone and everyone knew you, or so they thought. In small places like this, any difference sticks out like a sore thumb. From an early age, the reality of labels, gossip, and being picked on is quickly learned. You cannot avoid seeing this happening throughout your neighborhood and those around you. Without a doubt, I realized my vulnerability toward becoming one extremely sore thumb.

Growing up in a pint-sized farm community, life is routinely trial and error. There were no mentors or how-to guidebooks for my predicament. The most common mantra bestowed on me was "just do the best you can." Well-intentioned, this also meant that not much was expected of me. To counterpunch the stigma, I self-instilled the belief of eventually outgrowing this fiasco or being redeemed by some scientific breakthrough. If television could showcase a bionic man, reconstructed and refurbished, why then couldn't there be a high-tech solution for me as well?

My adolescent years left me no option but to adapt or else. For example, attending Catholic grade school required that I occasionally take my turn at the pulpit and lead the congregation in reciting the Epistle. Shortly before Mass, the parish priest would inform me of the passages to be read. In a momentary frenzy, I then quickly retreated to the sanctuary room, buried my face in the Holy Book, and memorized the assigned paragraphs. When it came time to stand at the podium and read, I did so with more than a prayer. Most likely, I could have been excused from this activity by pleading my case to the church pastor. However, doing so meant the risk of exclusion and lesser expectations. Therefore, I carried this same approach into the classroom.

This parochial era of mine resulted in varying reactions from the teachers. The nuns who taught here generally appeared sympathetic. The lay teachers seemed confused and frustrated.

Some even professed that I belonged elsewhere. One particular mentor, however, was both an adversary and an advocate. Ms. Irish, who boasted often of her Celtic heritage, was perhaps the most strict and stern among lay teachers. More formidable than even Ms. Alice, all that Ms. Irish required to establish control consisted of a few chosen words and harrowing stares. Her jet-black hair, ebony horn-billed glasses, and gloomy attire, added to Ms. Irish's ominous persona. The students who preceded me usually had plenty of embellished horror stories about this teacher, which personally affected me, due to the fact I lived directly across the street from her.

As the fifth grade and sometimes sixth grade educator, Ms. Irish set high standards for everyone and would settle for nothing less. Unlike the other teachers, who often fussed and fretted over my situation, Ms. Irish made no exceptions for me. I was simply expected to do as well as the rest of the class. Somewhat resentful at the time, I now see this teacher as my most influential instructor. Despite my unique circumstances, her expectations caused me to believe that I was equal to any challenge. Although often frightened by the demeanor of Ms. Irish, it is considerably scarier to think how I might have turned out if not for the lessons learned from this memorable lady.

Although these trials and tribulations sometimes sound a bit negative, a positive side burgeoned from my predicament. Never could I be accused of cheating. Eyeballing another's paper and copying the answers was not even a remote possibility. At the same time, my oversized handwritten responses were easily viewed by those around me. An ability to memorize and listen intently seemed heightened by the sheer need to keep pace.

Taunted by a fair share of bullies, teasing, and other school antics, one nemesis met my disdain, more so than all others. I hated blackboards and especially reviled those green varieties. They represented my greatest barrier and source of ridicule. Because of the lessons and pop quizzes placed upon them, I became destined to unthinkable acts. Throughout my earliest school years, I spent extensive time visiting the pencil sharpener during the chalked-on quizzes. Whenever the quiz questions could not be discerned, I improvised by walking over to the pencil sharpener located next to the blackboard and scanned the questions while endlessly sharpening another pencil. I whittled far too many pencils during this era.

As my education progressed and my vision did the opposite, other drastic means had to be adapted. A front row seat was customarily reserved for me among the brainy kids, where I definitely felt out of place. It also meant being separated from the more popular goof-offs, who ruled the back rows. This really irked those methodical teachers, who insisted on aligning classroom seating in an alphabetical order. Sometimes, I even transformed my desk into mobile furniture by carefully balancing it on my uplifted knees and then scooting just a little bit closer to the despicable blackboard.

When observing the blackboard from my up-front perch did not work, I was then instructed by the compromising teachers to walk up to the board and survey the questions point blank. This did wonders to draw increased attention to my situation and jeers from classmates, asking me to get out of the way. One teacher actually assigned me to sit at her desk in order to read the front blackboard assignments. This would occasionally result in several of the class clowns raising their hands and begging me to call on them. When lessons happened to be placed on the side blackboard, I then got directed to switch seats and force a fellow classmate to trade places. Of course, this imposed game of musical chairs never won favor with the disrupted student. All of this pretty much hampered any chances of blending in and avoiding freak show status.

My fourth grade teacher took great pride in meticulously scripting the day's lessons on both the front and side blackboards. Despite her immaculate penmanship and its considerable size,

I had to continually remind her that this just wasn't good enough for me. Sensing her resentment for the inconvenience this created, there were days when I dreaded going to school. Sometimes I didn't.

Some of the more enlightened educators gave me their written copy of the blackboard tests. However, this never happened until they were done transferring the material onto the board and handing it to me with just a fraction of class time remaining. Math teachers, in particular, usually had the answers attached to the sheet they were scripting from. Therefore, I had to wait even longer while they copied the math equations onto a separate sheet for me. The simplest accommodation was to have teachers verbalize the questions as they were being written on the blackboards. This occurred so inconsistently, that I oftentimes gave up and refrained from reminding them to do so. Occasionally, I would return after school to copy down blackboard assignments, only to find them already erased. Again, in these conundrum years, no one seemed to know how to deal with my situation and neither did I.

Life sure would have been a lot less stressful if computers, enhanced print and quality copiers existed at this time. Instead, I lived in the age of the carbon-copy mimeograph. Just about every test was printed on a mimeograph machine, which usually resulted in faded and blurred copies, especially those at the end of a run. Each time as the tests were being handed out, I went into anxiety mode while wondering whether I would get a legible copy. If not, I then had to ask for a better copy, only to be told that they all came out like this. And as always, there was that familiar advice, "Just do the best you can." Straining to read the tests often became so frustrating that I sometimes gave in to just guessing on multiple choice or true/false questions. This seemed to be good enough because, once again, not much was expected of me. At this rate, I often wondered whether my grades were actually based on achievement or a heavy dose of sympathy. Quite possibly, my passing marks may have also been influenced by no teacher wanting to hold me back and deal with my situation for another year.

Distant blackboards and pitiful print were far from my only obstacles. This town's version of the Beavis and Butthead characters routinely entertained themselves by calling out to get my attention. They would then flip me the finger and laugh, while I unknowingly waved back at their gestures. When I finally discovered what they were doing, I maliciously wanted to knock their brains out yet realized that someone had obviously done so already.

As previously noted, one of my most successful adaptations for fitting in was by memorizing. When it became my turn to read a passage from the textbook, I usually had it prerecorded in my brain cells. As classmates around me looked on and listened, I sat back peering at my book and then recited flawlessly the words on the page. The image of looking good, while reading well, seemed all so important. Infrequently, I would be tripped up and asked to read an unanticipated paragraph, thus creating instant panic, a hunched-over posture, and a struggling rendition. These varying Dr. Jekyll and Mr. Hyde presentations led some teachers to actually skip me when it came my turn to read out loud.

Sometimes in the midst of classroom life, I would get caught completely off guard. When spotted goofing around one day by Sister Coreen, she immediately called out my name and instructed me to read a paragraph from the textbook chapter she had been presenting. This was her payback for my not paying attention. As I looked down upon the textbook, my eyes strained to view the small print. Knowing that all thirty pairs of eighth-grade eyes were upon me, my ability to eyeball the sentences became even more unsettled by sheer nervousness. While stumbling along and sounding somewhat illiterate, desperation caused me to suddenly morph into a character role and continue my recitation by imitating a voice from the Bullwinkle and Rocky cartoon series. I guess this knee-jerk reaction was my way of creating a major distraction from the embarrassment now being executed through this reading. What happened next was just as unexpected. The ever so serious Sister Coreen lost control and burst into laughter. She then recomposed herself and directed me to discontinue reading. From this day forward, I had gained a new means to deal with adversity. When fun is potentially being poked your way, humor can counter as a deflector and diversion. As time progressed, I constantly required this approach to transform potential tragedies into comedies. At times, however, I just had to take my lumps in situations beyond my control.

Knowing that there were students in my class who had been held back one grade because of poor reading skills, I constantly feared the same consequence. This fate is what happened to Big John, whose setback then became regrettably associated with me. During a reading exercise, my teacher got so frustrated with Big John, that she openly chastised him and exclaimed, "Even Dan with his bad eyes reads better than you." Following this cockeyed comparison, neither Big John nor I ended this day with elevated esteems or a heightened friendship.

With the best of intentions, my eighth grade teacher took the initiative to obtain what was alleged as compatible large print textbooks. These supersized tutorials would not even fit in my modest desk. Herculean arms and strength were needed just to transport these monstrosities. Worse yet, the text inside often differed significantly from the standard classroom editions. And of course, these mutant books garnered far too much unwanted attention. I was more than content not to have these printed freaks define me during my forthcoming middle and high school years.

Even though all of us are said to be created equal, some seem more equal than others. The reminders become rudely evident during our grade school years. This is just that stage in life when comparisons begin and identities evolve. It is also a time when targets are being drawn and "good grief" moments occur. This scenario begins to peak during those treacherous middle school days. While enduring this junior high phase and anticipating that the next transition will warrant welcome changes, I dreamed of bigger and better things. Just like so many, however, I needed to discover that there can be looming senior high school nightmares as well. As such, everything instead got even less parochial, far more public, and considerably discombobulating.

Alas in Wonderland

In order to go from lemon to lemonade, some rigorous squeezing must be endured.

It would be much more dramatic to say that I took a flying leap and belly flopped into the mainstreams of middle school and high school. Sometimes it felt that way. The truth is, however, I waded in like everyone else and learned to sink or swim. While opting for the latter, the techniques I pursued were usually imaginative, oftentimes unconventional, and even desperate.

The transition from St. Joe's was complicated not only by my unique situation, but this also meant leaving behind a sacred and somewhat protective parochial environment. Adapting to the "publics" promised to be a whole new ball game with all kinds of strange and unfamiliar pitches. Pretty much confident that I could adjust to these new surroundings, in the back of my mind remained a lot of uncertainty as to whether everyone else could adjust to me.

My public middle school experience only involved the freshman year. Before I had any time to worry about this era, it had come and gone. Along with my fellow classmates, most of us seemed to be looking forward to high school with anticipations of driving, dating, drinking, and perhaps some academics. Although this time of dull classes in a dingy brick building was far from uneventful, not much about my middle school life seems memorable. Then again, perhaps the lingering horrors are so deeply suppressed that there can be no resurfacing of what really transpired. Somehow I survived this initiation into teendom and now headed to the high school promise land.

Similar to many small communities, my high school was

that gateway for eventually getting out of town. Withstand this stage and there will be something greater elsewhere. In the meantime, the walls, periphery, and inner sanctum of this educational enclave, served as a maze of teenage fantasies and misfortunes. Depending on how you adapted, high school was either an enchanting wonderland or an aimless wanderland. The twists and turns of this maze were just something you learn to navigate and tolerate. And hopefully, any and all dead ends were avoided.

To be quite honest, the concept of educational mainstreaming did not exist during my school years of the 1960's and early 1970's. Any student with different needs eventually disappeared within the system. If you had trouble making the grade, you were simply held back or banished to some obscure destination. During my high school experience, there was a mysterious end of the corridor room called B-5. This segregated haven housed what nowadays would be termed special education and related primarily to cognitive impairments. Almost secretive in nature, this place appeared to be a cloistered environment of shut-in students. Those associated with this classroom became tagged a "B-fiver." The blockhead bullies, of course, loved to antagonize their targets by chastising them with a B-fiver label.

As for students with major physical challenges, I cannot remember there being any others besides me enrolled in the mainstream of my school. There were no wheelchairs, white canes, hearing aids, oddball glasses, braces, crutches, or any signs of body language to indicate impairments or limitations. Among the community's youth, disability and invisibility seemed to go hand in hand. This reality, however, was simply a reflection of the times rather than of my particular hometown. Two examples of this conundrum became clear to me. A young boy, residing in my neighborhood, disappeared off to a distant school for the deaf. A few years later, my brother Tom moved two hours away to attend the state school for the blind. The only two hometown students, who seemed remotely close to my situation, had epilepsy, a subject only whispered about on occasion. Of course, this grapevine of whispers involved me as well.

Once again, nobody wants to be the sore thumb that sticks out. Unless commanded to read the small print or identify something at a distance, I blended in for the most part. Therefore, showcasing my unique situation never seemed like a good idea. From a high school perspective, you are less likely to fit in, if you are too far-out. At least that is how my teenage mentality deciphered this predicament. As long as they kept on shining, it need not be an issue that my faulty headlights were stuck on the low beams and slowly fading. What really mattered instead was directing just enough light on the road ahead. Nonetheless, hitting numerous potholes and crossing over the center line became a matter of habit for me.

My sophomore to senior years required the need to routinely reconfigure and fine-tune past approaches. Still, many of my former tactics continued on. The high school speech course mandated that each student perform a prepared reading in front of the class. For me this meant memorizing a three-page manuscript and rattling it off in Road Runner fashion. I still recall my teacher remarking that she had never before heard anyone read so fast. Then again, this was more of a less revealing recital than an actual reading. Nonetheless, this trade-off garnered a high grade while avoiding the classroom spectacle of planting my face in the text and stumbling along. Never underestimate the value of choreography as a means for fitting in.

Sometimes ingenuity fostered calamity. When it came to choosing between industrial arts or typing class, I opted for tool time. My first class began with demonstrations of table saws, band saws, routers, belt sanders, and drill presses. The bloody horror stories shared by the blunt instructor more than served as impressionable intimidation. After just two days in shop class, I decided to retain my life and limbs. A transfer to typing represented my only alternative. Now seated at the adjustable typing desk and straining to view the keyboard and training manual, I decided to modify this situation by cranking the center section of the typewriter stand to a height of closer visual proximity. While doing so, I had no idea that the power cord of my IBM Selectric was being squeezed by this innocent maneuver. Without warning, everything in the room shut down as a popping noise sounded and burning smell filled the air. No one seemed to know what was going on or how a circuit had been blown. After discretely cranking down my desk and departing with fellow students, I hurried out of the darkened room and began contemplating a return to shop class.

As for other classes, there were assorted challenges. I still don't know why my beaker jar blew up in chemistry class. Then again, I'm also not quite sure what comprised my chemical mixture because of those puny container labels and miniscule measuring devices. However, the safety glasses now made sense to me, yet did nothing to alleviate the need for close-up encounters with Bunsen burners, test tubes, and mysterious concoctions. Six weeks into this class, everything got even more perplexing when the longtime chemistry teacher suffered a fatal heart attack and passed away.

Needing to get into close range for biology lab dissecting, I nearly embalmed myself by inhaling a whole lot of nasty formaldehyde fumes. Within this process, I unmercifully mutilated several frogs and a sheep brain. As for that standard preserved piglet in the cutting tray, never could I be quite sure what my scalpel was slicing into or out of this poor sacrificial animal. Thank goodness for accommodating lab partners with better headlights.

Limited with options and again avoiding shop class, a drafting course tested my precision guesswork to measure up and figure out all the angles. The same applied to my geometry lessons. Having the same instructor for both of these classes, somehow this teacher got used to me. Immediately after posting any quiz questions on the blackboard, he would advance to my desk and recopy these same test questions onto my answer sheet. By all means, Mr. Polglaze really went the extra mile. Besides appreciating his efforts, I am also glad he did not resort to a supersized protractor and compass for my situation.

As for the utmost in academic irony, the mandatory driver's education class kept me steered in the right direction. At the same time, it sort of drove me crazy. Knowing that a driver's license would never be part of my future, this represented backseat driver's training at its finest. While classmates around me discussed their motoring prospects, I remained somewhat out of gear and never quite up to speed. Being the hitchhiker rather than the hot-rodder, a lack of wheels always served as my toughest high school hindrance. With road rage idling, my youthful cravings for the open highway sat stuck in neutral. It not only bugged me to beg for a ride but being unable to return the same favor also bothered me. In small places with no public transportation, driving is truly the teenage American dream.

In regard to extracurricular activities, somehow I managed to become the sports editor of the high school newspaper and a member of four different sports teams. By doing so, I experienced both the thrill of victory and the agony of defeat. Because the coaches were also classroom teachers of mine, they oftentimes finagled over my contrasts between athletics and academics.

During my free time, study halls constituted a mastery of clandestine protocol. Although I appeared to be loafing like so many fellow classmates, these sessions were perhaps my most productive hours. With crossed arms straddled on the desktop and my forehead resting upon them, I was actually reading my assignments at nose length. Being extremely sensitive to bright lighting, this also served as a shading strategy. From this perspective, it was far more acceptable to appear as a goof-off rather than a spectacle.

When my final year of high school came into play, it became time to begin future education and career planning. Toward the end of my senior year, a personal conference was arranged with the guidance counselor. Prior to the meeting, I did not have much interaction with this staff member. As best as I can recall, he was both new to this school and the profession. What I am really trying to say in a nice way, is that this guy was a legitimate greenhorn. During our meeting, he made it quite clear to me that my grades and personal situation as a nearsighted country hick would most likely make it extremely difficult for me to successfully complete college. When I asked him about other options, the conversation pretty much ended without any optimism. He appeared to be at a loss as to where I could venture next.

Sometimes you heed advice, and sometimes you don't. In contrast to this bleak outlook from the high school guidance counselor and assorted doubters, I went on to graduate from the nationally acclaimed business school at the University of Wisconsin-Whitewater and earned recognition from Who's Who Among Students in American Universities & Colleges. I also shared awards from the American Marketing Association, Associated Press, and Midwest Collegiate Outdoor Association. Perhaps it was defiance that drove me to prove the doomsayers wrong. Maybe it was my own gumption that kept me persevering. Quite possibly though, it was just an ongoing belief that you need not see everything around you as long as you catch a sufficient glimpse now and then.

Surviving high school was tough. There were days when I dreaded showing up for classes. However, I really cannot say that it was harder for me than anyone else. Surrounding me were classmates wishing to be a whole lot smarter, much taller, less chunky, more attractive, and just a little bit popular. As such, this high school of mine ended up with its fair share of freaks, geeks, dirtballs, eggheads, wannabe jocks, and nobodies, all of which made this experience far more enriching. In the midst of such company, I learned that it's sort of perfectly okay, to be somewhat imperfect.

Because of many reforms, schools nowadays deal more assertively in regards to students challenged by adversity. Assistive technology and sensitivity training have certainly brought changes. Nonetheless, contending with each others' differences will always remain a reality. If given a chance to relive my school days, I would probably do most of the same again. However, I sometimes shudder when thinking of how Power Point, iPods, laptops, and tiny cell phone texting would have impacted me during these formative years.

For Whom the Ball Rolls

Perhaps it is not just the way the ball bounces, but rather the opportunity to do so.

Never underestimate the value of sports and the competitive fire that burns within young athletes. This inferno need not be fueled solely by athletic ability but oftentimes just as much by the sheer desire to fit in and participate. In so doing, even a mere-sighted kid can race around ball diamonds, scrimmage on the gridiron, dribble down the court, and sprint to the finish line.

During my grade school years, no alternatives existed when it came to classes or playground politics. In the classroom, the lessons were the same for everyone. Outside this realm, recess rigmarole was no different. This routinely involved dividing into teams and playing softball or baseball. As a result, I quite often found myself positioned with a bat over home plate and awaiting a leather-covered ball to be hurled at me with lightening speed. It did not have to make sense to me or anyone else as to within what proximity I could actually see this approaching object. At my small Catholic school, everyone was needed to form teams and therefore, I took my turns both at the plate and in the outfield. While batting is considered offense, in my case, it was more a matter of timely defense. Instead of just swinging wildly and hitting the ball, my primary goal was always to prevent it from hitting me. By law of averages and a little luck, there were times when the ball actually struck my bat and popped into the playing field, at which point, I then dashed madly to first base with no idea as to whether the ball had been caught.

When it came to actually playing defense, I was always platooned to left field, where I could do the least damage as a real life Charlie Brown. If by chance the ball was hit my way, I usually had to guess its whereabouts according to the directions hollered by my team mates. By the time any ball reached my point of view, it was already racing past me. Perhaps that is why I was last to be picked when teams were formed. This playground selection process always established the tactless hierarchy as to where you fit in. Even though I loved sports, I absolutely despised the baseball diamond. When moving on to middle school and high school, it became a welcome relief to leave behind the mandatory malarkey of recesses on the baseball diamonds.

Early on, I had proven to be fleet of foot. One night while hanging out with friends at an American Legion baseball tournament, the hometown Jaycees sponsored a footrace after this game. A giant Babe Ruth candy bar served as the grand prize for winning in each age division. Having the combination of quick feet and a sweet tooth, I entered this event with a lot of motivation. To my good fortune, I indeed won. However, one of the local bullies decided he wanted possession of my Babe Ruth. By no means did I intend to relinquish my prize. Without hesitation, I again took off running with this thug rambling right behind me. While running for my life, I clutched the huge candy bar like a baton in a relay race. Prior to my bold dash, no one had dared to challenge this goon. After two spins around the park, the huffing and puffing dirtball finally gave up. While jogging away and munching on my chocolate treat, I became convinced of potentially having some notable athletic ability. Although running away from dire situations was not always an option, sometimes becoming a Speedy Gonzales or a Road Runner really had its advantages.

My freshmen through senior years represented new adventures, opportunities, and ordeals. I was glad to avoid baseball, yet nothing would stop me from taking shots at football, basketball, cross-country, and track. Throughout my earlier escapades on the playground, I did learn one thing. Any limitation in size, strength, or otherwise could be countered by speed, agility, and endurance. Apparently, one particular coach had a different perspective.

When freshmen football practice began, I showed up ready to play alongside my friends. After being issued a helmet, uniform, and pads, I rushed out onto the field and lined up with the rest of the team. What happened next, I had not anticipated. One by one, each player got queried as to what position he was trying out for. When it came my turn, I proudly proclaimed "running back." In response, the coach walked up to me, paused momentarily, and then loudly inquired, "You're that kid with bad eyes, aren't you?" Emphasizing that I could not play this position, he then directed me to join the linemen. Good grief, I had just been downgraded from Charlie Brown to a combination of Daffy Duck and Mr. Magoo. Having no time to dwell on whether this was an insult or acceptance, I directed my imposing five foot nine and 130-plus pound physique toward the more prominently framed linemen. Again, being part of a small school, just about everyone is needed to muster full-fledged freshmen, junior varsity, and varsity football teams. Ready and willing to play almost any position, I mostly excelled at warming the bench. Even though I proved to be one of the better punters, this was quickly ruled out for fear I might lose sight of the ball in the process.

As a not-so-ominous offensive lineman, my assignments involved shielding the quarterback and blocking for running backs. To this day, I still recall my first scrimmage against the varsity. Late in the practice, I was finally called upon to replace a beat-up teammate. After racing out on to the field and lining up, I discovered my challenge involved blocking a senior everyone fondly referred to as Chocolate. At six feet seven, not only did Chocolate tower over me, but he also exceeded my weight by at least a hundred pounds. I felt like a Volkswagen Beetle about to be hit head-on by a Mach truck. Thank God for gentle giants. Just as the play unfolded, a motoring Chocolate burst across the line, swung his right arm around my chest, lifted me off the turf, and proceeded chasing the quarterback while carrying me along for the ride. This should have stymied my football pursuits, yet I somehow kept playing for three seasons until a nasty broken arm and torn ligaments ended my ambitious gridiron days.

When it came to track, the results were quite the opposite. Even an out of sight football player can manage to run around in circles while following white lines. For me, that translated into the 440yard dash, 880 yard run, mile relay, and an occasional half-mile relay. However, my low-flying attempts to reach new heights as a high jumper never did pan out. By my senior year, I had sprinted well enough to already letter twice and be named co-captain as the track season began. This time, speed and endurance counted. However, neither track nor football was my first sports love. Like that of my closest friends, basketball beckoned more than any other athletic challenge.

In this rural community of less than four thousand, basketball reigned supreme. My scrawny school scripted an epic "David versus Goliath" story when its hometown team beat the big-city Milwaukee boys for the state high school title. At the time, no separate divisions existed according to school size. Having beaten the incredible odds to win this championship, every young boy in this town grew up striving to be part of this same legacy, and I was no exception.

My basketball escapades began on the driveway of Clyde's house. His real name was Steve, yet following a transition of a half-dozen nicknames, he became Clyde. At the end of his driveway was a small detached garage. Its sloping roof required the netted rim to be placed at a much lower height than usual. As such, an improvised game got created using a volleyball that could be easily cupped with one hand and slam-dunked. With practice and a little luck, you could even bank the ball off the angled overhang. This cockamamie court became our local version of quasi-pro basketball.

While at St. Joe's, I joined the eighth grade basketball team. Due to the limited resources of this holy setting, there was a shortage of uniforms. As such, I was only able to play every other game due to sharing a uniform with another player. In this league of only a handful of games each season, I still remember scoring my one and only basket on a precision hook shot. At this juncture, I loved the sport, yet felt somewhat unsure of my ability to play at the forthcoming public school level. Big bad Arnie, however, helped to change that.

Throughout the next summer, I started upgrading my shooting and dribbling at a driveway court located next door to my grandpa's Citgo gas station. This concrete pad, with its freestanding backboard and rim, was built by its owner so that his son could hone his basketball skills. Now that his son had grown and moved on, this hoop became available for any of the neighborhood kids who wanted to work on their game.

While practicing one balmy evening on this outdoor court, a tall kid nicknamed Arnie approached me. Arnie was not someone I normally associated with. He had the well-established reputation of being a nasty dude and often hung out with the local dirtballs, who spent most of the summertime sitting on the courthouse steps and smoking cigarettes. This guy was definitely someone I learned to steer clear of. However, now as Arnie drew closer, I feared the worst.

Staring down at me, Arnie commanded, "Toss me that ball." Pondering this demand, I then envisioned him walking away with my cherished basketball. Taking off and running did not seem to be my option this time. Instead, the choice facing me now was quite simple, either give up the basketball or my life. Just as I forfeited the ball, Arnie caught me off guard by saying, "How about we play a little one-on-one?" As such, I now realized that instead of pummeling me outright, he was going to slowly torture me on this cement court. However, this notorious character not only showed off his athletic skills, but also, began mentoring me throughout the game. After giving me pointers on my jump shots, Arnie taught me some new moves around the basket. Following an hour of basketball skirmishes and two games of horses, Arnie indicated that he needed a smoke and took off toward the courthouse. As he left, this notorious character walked over to the far end of the court, picked up a long-bladed knife, and replaced it back into his right boot. As the summer wore on, only once more did he stop by for another game of buckets. Thanks to Arnie, my game improved and so did my confidence in trying out for the freshman team.

Apart from witnessing him at a few school cafeteria and parking lot fights, I saw little of Arnie throughout middle school and high school. Between skipping out and being suspended, he was more often absent than present. Arnie could have been one of the school's best athletes, but that would have meant rules and restrictions. It is really amazing how one or two encounters can form an impression. After going one on one with this big, bad dude, I gained a lot of respect for Arnie. Whenever others talked down about him, I wanted to jump in and say otherwise. However, I did not wish to soften such a hard-earned and hardcore reputation.

During the middle school and high school noontime lunch breaks, I became one of those wannabe jocks who skipped the cafeteria and dashed straight to the gym for a half hour of buckets. Once the lunch break bell sounded, the other hoopster crazies and I then headed back to the classrooms, dripping in sweat and anticipating the same routine the next day. It was an accepted macho price to pay for these daily athletic heroics and set us apart from those sissies who spent their free time rehearsing with the band. Besides all this, we got to hear, over and over again, the same Black Sabbath, Alice Cooper, and Joe Cocker albums blasting away in the gym each day.

Unlike football and track, basketball was more limited as to who made the freshman, junior varsity, and varsity teams. This meant three strings and fifteen uniforms at each level. At the start of the season, tryouts usually involved twenty or so hopefuls for each team. As a cruel reality, this translated into a handful of players being cut. No matter how tough a character you pretended to be, experiencing the axe definitely whacked a hard blow to the ego. However, what seemed even worse to some was getting beat out by the kid who left nose prints on his textbooks. In many ways, I understood their frustration. It made no sense to me either how I differed from the classroom to the ball court. Limited in my central vision and relying more on the peripheral, I played a scrappy cockeyed game that focused more on movements than details. Utilizing speed and reflexes, I managed to get in the way of the opposing player, cut off passes, and retrieve loose balls. When it came to shooting, I simply aimed the ball toward the middle of that huge white backboard. Apparently all of this was just good enough for me to become a venerable member of the freshmen and junior varsity "Scrubs."

Only a select five were annually accepted into this infamous basketball brotherhood. During my affiliation, Terry, Kent, Jim, and Steve were fellow Scrubs. The title bestowed both notoriety and distinction. Although relegated as perennial third-string benchwarmers, we considered ourselves more like legends. In a category of our own, we were the last to make the team, last to be inserted into the game, and, of course, always last to be recognized for our talents. To compensate, the five of us adopted the Scrubs title as a badge of honor.

As for me, I pretty much considered myself the Scrub of Scrubs. Not being among the tallest or the strongest of hoopsters, I depicted a lousy rebounder with little leaping ability. My ball handling needed more than considerable improvement. When it came to shooting, I never quite matched my scoring aspirations. Out of sync on depth perception, I constantly got caught up in foul play and sometimes completely missed crosscourt passes. Adding to my less than stellar acuity, it could be said that I was more than fortunate to even be part of any game. Nonetheless, all that mattered was envisioning what to do whenever the ball got within my view.

Being a Scrub, I shared good company. There were valid reasons why the five of us accumulated so much bench time. Our entries onto the court usually came when the scoreboard showed the team way ahead or hopelessly behind. On rare occasions, some Scrubs got thrust into the games early, whenever the coach needed to motivate any slacking starters. We accepted these roles and became a close-knit fraternity with our own set of unwritten rules. Dare not to become too good or you could relinquish this stalwart status. We also had an understanding that if any of us were sent into the competition and got our hands on the ball, attempting shots would take priority over giving the chance to anyone else. As a Scrub, scoring opportunities were few and far between, therefore, making the scoring charts was the ultimate reward. Besides, Scrub scores always served as a crowd-pleaser.

The quintessential roles played by Scrubs are sadly misunderstood and unappreciated. From our courtside perches, we more often serve as the cheerleaders, rather than the cheered. Throughout the grind of daily practices, it is the Scrubs' dull resistance which sharpens the starters' skills and bolsters their confidences. As die-hard apprentices yearning forever to be the mentors, we Scrubs dutifully took on the demanding task of making everyone around us look better.

My reputation as a Scrub was indeed different than most others. The "bad eyes" connotation carried over from football. Therefore, some classmates of mine decided to make my basketball game more interesting by christening me "Radar." It was their way of explaining how an optically off-kilter kid could play this sport. On those rare occasions, when I entered the game and attempted a shot, the cheered, "bleep, bleep, bleep" to mimic a radar signal. While many made this their moment of laughter, I was not humored by the hysterics. However, it was indeed a part of the out of bounds territory I had chosen to compete in. Perhaps this up and down the floor effort relegated me to basketball court jester, which, when you think about it, sort of creates an association with royalty.

Some of us are gamers and some are not. There were always critics who questioned my involvement in competitive sports. Others simply gave me a sporting chance. During my four years of middle and high school sports, like all athletes, I was required to pass an annual physical exam. My doctor was a close friend of the family and well-acquainted with my situation. Foregoing the standard eye exam, he instead penciled in a figure that made my visual acuity less alarming. This represented a down home version of reasonable accommodation. As a backup plan, however, I had already memorized enough lines on the standard eye chart to garner a sufficient rating.

The middle and high school eras can be trying times, especially for anyone who enters the mainstream with any kind of limitation. This automatically creates a target. I never relished the "Radar" chant during my time on the hardwood floors. No reminder was required as to my eyes not being up to par. Most definitely, I did not need another label. Then again, I had game and a uniform, while those in the bleachers were nothing more than bystanders. As such, score one for the kid with bad eyes, a feisty attitude, and Road Runner feet, all of which manifested a legendary Scrub, and one for whom the ball rolls.

A Christmassy Carol

When attempting to be like everyone else, each of us is far too unique to be anyone else.

Around my modest hometown, being known as the "kid with bad eyes" was by no means a desirable distinction. In small places, any shortcoming becomes more of a distraction than an attraction. Unfortunately, my limited acuity simply did not measure up to that of others, and thus, there donned this somewhat accurate, yet unwanted label. No one seemed to understand my situation. To make matters worse, neither did I.

Denial or acceptance of this predicament was not a choice. However, I did not have to like it and never have. This unsightly inconvenience just got in the way of too many teenage things that needed doing. When it came to academics and athletics, my survival relied on sight unseen and a fair amount of cockamamie creativity. Somehow, this almost leveled the playing field. Nonetheless, it was never enough. As a young man, what I really coveted most of all were four wheels and a little romance.

As my freshman year ended, so did my in-town residence. Yearning for that country living, my family moved just over three miles north of town. Although I loved the great outdoors and now lived directly across from a five thousand acre state park with two lakes, access to town and friends suddenly became an ongoing struggle. Deprived the independence of a driver's license and residing a fair distance from teenage civilization, this dilemma translated into a logistical nightmare. Being out of sight, as well as out of town, created a long and winding road to dances, movies, parties, and just hanging out. These hurdles required leaps of faith, persuasive ride mooching, and lengthy walks.

At this stage in my life, I was really not sure what to make of myself and equally uncertain as to how others perceived me, especially the opposite sex. My oddball classroom strains and struggles certainly did not score positive points. The contrasts between the classroom, athletics, and other endeavors, only fostered confusion. Adding to this quandary, my lack of direct eye contact often got interpreted as an unfriendly, insecure, or uninterested persona. Catching the eye of another was the aim of this game, whose rules I could not follow like everyone else. As an anxious teenager, I continually pondered as to whether the way I saw the world around me could actually be overlooked.

Because this was the age of Beatlemania and mop-tops, fitting in required a certain look from the top down. Like most of my peers, I beckoned my hair to tumble toward my shoulders. In my case, this crown of mine flopped like a frizzled tug-of-war. As hard as I tried to straighten it and increase its length, the natural curls fought back tenaciously. Adding to this discontent, I could never quite accomplish the macho matching sideburns during my high school days. However, I was not to be denied the trendy attire of these times.

Digressing for a moment, let's just say that a totally incognito fit within the mainstream isn't absolutely necessary. As much as I wanted to blend in, my rebellious non-conformist side craved liberation. Influenced by the sounds of rock and roll, my generation aspired for a radical look. This more than suited me. Impressionable as a teenager, I focused intensely on the fashions and evolving styles of the psychedelic 1970's. In my case, I strived to be just at the edge of the mainstream. Therefore, be mindful that my middle and high school years were sandwiched between the hippie and disco movements, making me an inevitable victim of both these eras.

When everyone else donned the trendy dark-blue CPO

jackets, the one covering me had to be burgundy instead. During the Beatle-inspired craze of groovy Nehru shirts, white dickeys, and tacky medallions, mine became a silky green paisley version. While friends strutted about in navy pea coats and air force snorkel parkas, the military look for me included an army "Ike" jacket of WWII vintage. My safari jacket, with its multiple pockets and backside belt, was nothing less than cool. For formal occasions, I actually owned a polyester leisure suit, which escaped the closet only once. A blue hound's-tooth blazer, complimented by a white clip-on necktie, showcased in my senior year picture. The deep-purple bell bottoms, discovered at the funky Chess King store in Madison, got accented by a three inch wide white double buckle belt. These leggings couldn't be missed as I wandered the high school hallways. Prior to this pair of pants came the pinstriped flares and ballooned-sleeved shirt from the Monkeys collection in the Sears catalog.

Although my wide-wale corduroy Ponderosa shirt and gladiator watch band were nothing special, nobody had anything as "far-out" as my high-cut denim hippie shoes with jute laces. Eventually, I got even cooler by donning faded bib overalls. To this day, I still agonize over the hijacking of my fleece-collared bomber jacket during a local dance. Luckily, that temptation to own one of those suede buckskin coats with the fringed sleeves never came to fruition. Instead, bravado led to a letter jacket with a big *"D"* sewn on it. This curious teenage costuming of mine, however, paled in comparison to that of the stylish gals around me.

There is no denying the heavy burden that acceptance represents. At no time in a young man's life does this loom more critically than during the high school dating scene. Looking good and being able to look about go hand in hand. If that is not clear, let me put it this way. For adequate sightseeing, you need adequate sight and sites for seeing. As my freshman to senior years coincided with the flirtatious miniskirt craze, twenty-

twenty acuity was far from necessary to stir the burgeoning emotions of any teenage guy. I wholeheartedly plead guilty to frequent glances and even a few sustained stares. Quite frankly, those radically heightened hemlines created more eyestrain for me than blackboards. By no stretch of the imagination, does it need to be explained why ascending the long school stairways between classes, became a source of cherished entertainment.

During a pep rally week, I still vividly recall when a female classmate asked to borrow my orange and black school T-shirt. A couple of days later, she and several other girls came to class dressed only in these shirts. Reacting to this show of school spirit, even my social studies teacher, Mr. Rukauf, appeared visibly distracted on this day. Perhaps I could survive this era without wheels, but never without some interaction concerning that other gender.

Like most youthful guys in the early stages of interacting with equally young gals, I was both interested and intimidated. Of course, the always looming possibility of rejection terrified me. Overcoming this fear took some prodding and a most fortunate phone connection. My friend Kirk first got me started by letting me in on the real secret to communicating with the opposite sex. His discovery opened up a whole new world to me. Quite simply, Kirk knew of the only pay phone in town, where upon dropping in a dime and dialing, this same dime would always be returned at the end of the call. The only requirement consisted of a slight whack to the right spot on the side of the pay phone. Not only did this mean unlimited calling, it also meant complete privacy within this coveted phone booth. Oddly enough, the defective pay phone was located just outside the telephone company building. In this era of party lines and wall-mounted kitchen phones, liberation from eavesdropping transpired into the ultimate teenage freedom.

Despite the faulty headlights, I saw well enough to differentiate between the good, the bad, and the ugly. Sorry, but that is just telling it like it is. We each have our parameters and preferences. None of us are immune from scrutiny or seduction, and so it was in my freshman year when, I joined an entire league of fellow admirers who had a crush on a classmate named Carol. She was perhaps the most personable, most attractive, and probably the most perfect girl in our school. Along with her sidekicks, Jackie and Pam, her clan was commonly referred to as our version of "Charlie's Angels." There was simply no way not to have a crush on Carol, and so I did.

As an optimist, I dreamed about having a girlfriend like Carol, yet, as a realist, never truly anticipated the possibility. If someone like Carol were to even greet me and acknowledge my existence, this would surely be more than enough. To this day, I am still not sure how it happened, but Carol and I eventually became good friends. I often sat next to her in study hall and even got to walk her home on one occasion. Although Carol dated some of the most popular guys in school, she always took the time to treat me as her friend. This of course, was a classic case of teenage infatuation and the haphazard distraction of attraction. Regardless of whom we are or want to be, all young hearts are susceptible to such an affliction.

Just before the winter holiday season, I was confronted with the most horrible news. Carol and her family were moving immediately to another town. Because of her dad's job transfer, the distance between us would soon tally over fifty miles. This teenage shock wave delivered a crushing blow to an endearing crush. Without a driver's license in my future, I would probably never get the chance to take an extended cruise and see her again. As holidays rolled around, I was still bummed about the departure of my friend. Just the day before Christmas, however, a card addressed to me arrived in the mail. It was from Carol, and for the first time in my awkward young adult life, I received a Christmas card from a girl. It was like teenage heaven to me.

Although downtrodden by Carol's relocation, I resorted to the only thing a rookie romantic could do. When one crush moves away, you just move on to the next one, perhaps one more after that, and possibly another, for good measure. This only becomes a dilemma based on supply and demand, along with a whole lot of what-ifs and wishful thinking.

As a teenager with any shortcoming, you wonder about your potential and prospects. Even the toughest of characters cannot always barrel through the barriers. Feeling so much peer pressure often leads to some dark moments, yet it is incredible how enlightening just one act of kindness can become. From the very day I received Carol's card, my attitude, esteem, and ambitions got a booster shot. If someone like me was good enough to get a special greeting from someone so perfect, perhaps I was considerably less imperfect than I realized.

The rest of my high school days had their ups and downs. After overcoming more than a few rejections, I experienced my share of dates. Because transportation always remained an issue, this often transpired to relying on double-dating. As a result, this meant that my date and I were always relegated to the back seat. That, however, is another tantalizing story I am not quite ready to share.

To prove I could be just as deviant as any other teenager, I readily participated in the Piggly Wiggly watermelon raids. At the Dodge Theater, harassing poor old Otto became part of my antics. During the summer months, my fair share of firecrackers, cherry bombs, and M-80's got ignited. Water balloon bombardments served as a local ambush routine. Along with fellow rabble-rousers, I frequently snuck into the middle school under the cover of darkness. There may have also been one incident involving a smoke bomb in the lobby of the Higby Hotel. However, booze, drugs, and fights were fortunately absent from these scenes.

Despite the sad-sack impressions of my teenage years, I am not quite sure that this era was any worse for me than for others. There were times when I hung out with the coolest guys like Rock, Terry, and Robin. Clyde let me tag along as his hunting and fishing buddy. Along with characters named Warthog, Rooster, Skunk, and Moon Duck, I loitered outside of Kelly's Pool Hall. Oftentimes, I joined in on card games at Butt and Cubby's basement. I was even invited to one of Jackie's crazy parties. Somehow, I usually managed to hitch a ride to Midway Lanes. Some of the tough dudes, like Kloss, Munster, and Chi-Town, backed me up when needed. Kent, Carl, and Scott accompanied me from high school to the same college. And then there was my best friend, Larry, without whom I would have missed a whole lot of dances, parties, bowling alley rendezvous, and carload cruising. Looking back, it seems that the entire hometown gang was watching out for me. As such, regardless of some funky threads, the faulty headlights, and a lack of wheels, I got by with a little help from my friends

Call to the Wild

As long as you maintain your aim, it does not matter where your sights are set.

It is now safe to go back into the woods. No longer are there shots in the dark. The shadowy recluse who once prowled over hill and dale has been disarmed. All wild critters, furry and feathered, can again roam freely. Finally relinquished are the scattered doses of fatal lead poisoning. At long last and forevermore, though it did not come easy, I gave up on hunting.

Not everything has to make sense, nor even be rational. Certain things are simply instinctive and sometimes a rite of passage. Take for example my passion for the hunt and its related adventures. Growing up in a rural community often translates into two seasons, fishing and hunting. Surrounded by woods, scattered brush fields, and numerous waterways, it becomes tough to fit in without pursuing the great outdoors. For many a young boy, this serves as your first step into manhood. Therefore, you take up the cause, muster some bravado, and join deep-rooted traditions. Although not everyone is afflicted with an outdoorsman fever, many are often born with it. I was no exception. Fueled by the local culture and enormous stacks of *Field & Stream, Outdoor Life, and Sports Afield* magazines, I saw no reason not to get hooked or take up arms.

When it comes to fishing and hunting, there really is only one major difference. You need not see the fish in order to succeed. On the other hand, hunting requires a certain level of acuity. From my perspective, that did not mean twenty-twenty vision. As such, I heavily armed myself as a teenager and literally shot off into the woods. Doing so only required a few classroom sessions and a seasonal hunting license. Being somewhat out of sight was not really a matter for concern. If this sounds somewhat absurd and altogether dangerous to you, just consider that it simply added to the excitement of the hunt.

Despite my particular situation, it never occurred to me that I should not hunt. In my case, it just meant getting closer to the prey or pursuing bigger game. Apparently, the same logic persisted with my hunter safety instructor. Here in Wisconsin, anyone under the age of sixteen years old must first pass a hunter's safety course in order to obtain a license and hunt without adult supervision. Therefore, along with several friends, I signed up and attended the class. After paying close attention and passing the written exam, I proceeded to the shooting range for my final test. Once the class was lined up and facing the targets, each student was given our first round of ammunition and instructed to commence firing. After several rounds, I was approached by the perplexed instructor, who noted that my small game target had not once been hit. During a brief conversation, I then hinted about having a minor problem with zeroing in on the tiny target. While my instructor began hemming and hawing for a few minutes, I braced for the inevitable doom of failing completely. However, what came next still surprises me. The instructor walked to the end of the shooting range and posted a huge archery target. He then returned, hesitated for a moment, and told me to try again. It worked and I passed, with somewhat less than flying colors.

Although one hurdle had been overcome, others were to follow. By no means would I ever evolve into a sharpshooter with precise accuracy. For this reason, I discovered the shotgun. The blaster in my possession was a .20 gauge bolt-action Savage, containing a three-shot clip. In terms of small game hunting, you could call this scattergun a bazooka. While my squirrel hunting buddies carefully lined up the sights of their puny .22 caliber rifles, my point of view only required aiming in the general direction. During one late September outing, it became my turn to first shoot a treed bushy-tail. After conferring with my fellow hunters as to just where that squirrel was located, I chambered a two and a half inch Winchester shell loaded with #6 lead and fired away. My first thundering shot blew off all the leaves above the squirrel. The next shot eliminated all the leaves and a few branches below it. As this poor creature hunkered down in the crotch of the tall oak, I sensed the impatience of my buddies. Suddenly from behind me, a .22 crackled sharply, and down tumbled the squirrel. At least, someone had prevailed, even though I was pretty sure my third shot would have done the same.

Based on this experience and similar awkward encounters, my preference was to hunt solo. I suspect that others appreciated this scenario as well. Living across the road from a five thousand acre state park, I had ready access to the vast woodlands adjacent to this public wildlife refuge. Not being truly adept at spotting and stalking, I usually planted myself deep in the woods, sat quietly as possible, and waited for the game to come to me. Even though lesser territory got covered, this approach led to many a wild and wooly encounter. Sit long enough in the woods, and suddenly it becomes more alive than you can imagine. While many of the local hunters only caught sight of squirrels, rabbits, grouse, and deer, my confrontations included more elusive critters such as bobcats, weasels, coyotes, owls, possums, muskrats, skunks, badgers, and foxes. At least, I am pretty sure that's what they were. I still fondly recall observing an otter family along Mill Creek, yet no one else around here seems to ever have seen the same. Then there was that time when I impulsively decide to test the tenacity of a leaning hollow tree. Appearing ready to tumble, all that remained of this decaying tree was a seven-foot-high trunk. In an effort to help it along, I gave it a hardy push, and to my surprise, the roots gave way and the tree toppled downward. As it struck the ground, the entire trunk shattered into kindling. In the midst of all this, a befuddled raccoon rumbled out while shaking his head. With an unappreciative snarl, he then vamoosed off into the underbrush. Regrettably, I had not meant to be a home wrecker. Later this same day, I came upon another decrepit tree with a sizable hole in its trunk. As I peered inside this opening, several pairs of eyes stared back at me. Not wanting to create another homeless situation, I left this family alone and wandered away.

Also to be recollected is that dense foggy morning, while sitting on a brushy slope, the earth suddenly began moving uphill in my direction. Slowly but surely, something cryptic crawled beneath the autumn leaves and headed in my direction. At the exact same time, a loud shrieking noise reverberated from the swampy lowlands nearby. It resembled a death cry of sorts. On came the goose-bumps, as the hazy

surroundings amplified the spooky sights and sounds. For assurance, I clutched my loaded shotgun. Mesmerized by the obscured life force advancing toward me, I froze in place for what seemed like an eternity. Closer and closer, the undercover motion crept forward. Once again, the shrieking sound echoed off to my left. However, my main concern remained focused on the unimpeded threat now within just a few feet of me.

With the shotgun resting upon my lap, I debated whether to slide my finger back on its safety and betray my motionless stance. This entranced state of mine got interrupted when my right hand instinctively grabbed a nearby stick. Apprehensive at first, I finally reached out toward the movement and cleared away the rustling leaves. Hidden under them was a less than lethal box turtle on its final expedition before dozing off into hibernation. As for that other eerie anomaly, I stayed put and left well enough alone.

Within the fields and forests, there are many strange things, especially at both dusk and dawn. Having witnessed so many unusual critters, I was fairly sure that eventually I would be one of the first to spot a black bear in this neck of the woods. The old-timers swore that a few evasive bruins use to roam this region. On restless occasions, I often scanned the surrounding landscape with my binoculars, an old dime store pair that never seemed to focus quite right. During a deep woods outing into a previously unexplored area, my subpar 7 x 35 lens caught sight of a vague and crouched figure in the distant underbrush. Stepping carefully and quietly, the stalking ensued. Straining through the binoculars, I periodically zeroed in on the mysterious silhouette. Because this was deer hunting season, I now carried a heavy duty .30-06 Springfield, chambered with 200 grain hollow points. As such, I was armed to ambush anything in the wilds. Drawing closer, it finally became time to awaken whatever it was that lurked motionless in hiding. My finger then slid backward to release the safety. Should this thing decide to attack, I would be ready. Moments later, the stealth effort abruptly ended without a shot being fired. Somehow the beast had escaped, and all that remained near his hideout was an old rotting stump. Curses, foiled again.

To stretch the season, I also took up bow hunting. This close range endeavor seemed more in tune with my unique skills. Besides, I had already proven my ability to hit an archery target. However, it was one particular bow-hunting event that almost caused me to give up the outdoors altogether. While taking a shortcut across a pasture, I had no concerns about what seemed to be a docile herd of grazing cattle. Suddenly, these usually mild-mannered cows became ticked off by my trespassing and stampeded directly toward me. Making a beeline for the nearby fence, I barely cleared the top barbed-wire strand as the hell bent Holsteins homed in on me. High jumping a thorny fence with a bow and razor-sharp arrows in hand is not a feat I ever wish to attempt again. However, it takes more than one near casualty to quell the hunting spirit.

Do not underestimate the magic of this call to the wild, especially for any school kid burgeoning into a young hunter. Whenever held hostage in the classroom on a brisk October day, nothing is more liberating than an after-school hunt alongside your buddy and his dad. With just a few hours of sunlight remaining, you head out of town to that favorite squirrel woods. Upon entering this haven, every sense heightens. When first pausing to listen for any telltale critter sounds, you are momentarily overcome by the earthy smell of damp leaves matting the ground. While cradling the smooth wood stock of your gun and carefully gliding your finger over the cold steel trigger guard, you then trek slowly ahead and begin scanning the half-naked treetops. Some are already stripped completely of their fall foliage, which, to your advantage, eliminates the lofty hiding places.

By the time you reach the distant end of the woods, the bare-boned trees and their shadows have grown more sinister. The early setting of the autumn sun and the cool air descending upon you issues a bleak reminder of the oncoming season of snow and ice. Twilight now signals that it is time to retreat from this wilderness. In the fading light, you look to the left, then to the right, and finally to the thick groves behind you. Unexpectedly, it is discovered that your hunting partners are nowhere in sight. Either they meandered to the other side of the hill or already hiked out of the woods.

While carrying the day's bounty in one hand and a gun in the other, you carefully retrace the steps that brought you this far. In this enclave of darkness, the sounds of the emerging night creatures unsettle the murky surroundings. Shielded by the blackening turnabout, these nocturnals now have the edge. Your pace suddenly quickens as it becomes possible that you are the haunted and the hunted. Feeling vulnerable, your grip tightens firmer on the gun, and the pace escalates again. Every root on the forest floor seems to reach out and snag your feet. Just as you become unsure of the direction taken, a nearby automobile horn blasts out the needed bearings. Upon reaching the car and heading homeward, the rapid breathing finally subsides. However, your imagination continues to peak as the next hunt is pondered. You can hardly wait until then.

Over many fall and winter seasons, I remained an avid hunter but not so successful a shooter. Confound it, this transformed me into somewhat of an Elmer J. Fudd chasing "wascally wabbits." It mattered little to me. I was in this for the hunt rather than the kill. My entire lifetime take of squirrels, rabbits, and one unfortunate grouse, does not merit bragging nor does that episode when I silenced an annoying crow. Throughout my years of deer hunting, I managed three shots and three misses with a gun and also an identical three shots and three misses with my bow. The closest anyone in my family came to scoring a deer was when a ten point buck broadsided my dad's Oldsmobile and broke its neck. In the midst of the rut, this anxious buck had been pursuing a flirtatious doe across Highway 23. The doe barely missed dad's front bumper while the big buck fatally crashed head-first into the left front fender. Although DNR regulations allowed my dad to claim and keep this deer, he instead donated it to a family out of work and needing meat for the table.

So intense was the passion or perhaps obsession for hunting that I quit the high school cross-country team in my senior year. The practices and weekend meets stole away just too much valuable autumn time. Looking back, this still remains one of those lifetime regrets as this team went on to win the state championship. In my sophomore year, my English class term paper chronicled the history of Colt firearms, whereas my junior year speech presented a keynote address on the environmental benefits of hunting. Like a lot of high school kids in this region, I took great pride in skipping classes during deer hunting season. Showcasing a look of bravado, some of us came fashionably late to the classroom in our blaze orange. For a while, I aspired to someday become a game warden, as if that made any sense. The local poachers would have loved it immensely. Even the idea of falconry got toyed with, which probably would have been the most practical of my predatory ambitions.

My towering stacks of outdoor magazines led to dreams of big game Alaskan and African safaris. Sojourning southward for a wild boar or jaguar hunt would have been really cool as well. On rainy weekends, I sometimes spent an entire day scanning the magazine ads to learn about new rifles, different kinds of ammunition, reloading equipment, animal call systems, and government surplus bargains. After responding to an *Outdoor Life* ad from Ozark Mountain Kennels, I almost considered raising Black & Tan, Bluetick, and Redbone coonhounds as a moneymaking venture. Adding to these delusions, I enrolled in a mail-order taxidermy course in anticipation of mounting my own future trophies. Unfortunately, this hapless pursuit never progressed beyond a deformed pigeon and a rotting northern pike.

Narrated by Curt Gowdy, *The American Sportsman* ranked ahead of *Hogan's Heroes, Combat, I Spy, and Star Trek* as my favorite TV show. Hyped up by this ABC broadcast, I would then visit the local True Value hardware store just to gaze at the long row of Remingtons, Winchesters, Marlins, Mossbergs, and Savages. Perhaps someday, I might actually own a prized over-and-under Beretta shotguns or even a custom Weatherby rifle with a variable-power Redfield scope.

To further these shenanigans, I even involved my paternal grandmother. As a present for my fifteenth birthday, I persuaded her to purchase me a membership in the Outdoor Life Book Club. New members were awarded three free books chosen by the club. When mine arrived, this bonus package included a publication titled *The Sex Life of Animals.* Upon inspection by my Bible-abiding mother, this educational and illustrated book got confiscated immediately. Of course, this was nothing that a teenage boy would be interested in anyway. Besides, the other two books had much more valuable information such as how to identify wild game tracks and survive Grizzly bear attacks.

Like so many young hunters of this era, my shooting ventures began in the backyard with a cherished BB gun. Mine was a legendary Daisy Model 94. This lever action elevated me to Wild-West status. Equipped with such a trusty firearm, I was able to ward off the outlaw gangs of pestilent pigeons, which ravaged my neighborhood. My entry into real firepower came when Uncle Homer lent me an old single shot .22 to purge the cow pastures of gophers.

Eventually, my arsenal would graduate to a couple of .22s, a shotgun, and a large caliber deer rifle. To this day, I still regret not being able to add a Winchester.30-.30 to my collection. It also would have been an absolute asset if high-powered scopes and barrel tapping had been affordable for me.

Eventually, several events happened that began to curb my hunting passion. On separate outings, I felt like the targeted prey as errant high caliber bullets whizzed dangerously close to me. Experiencing the whirling sound of an approaching bullet and its impact into a nearby tree goes well beyond unnerving. Although it was fair game to question my personal acuity, I became well acquainted with too many trigger-happy knuckleheads, who shot at anything that moved or spitefully fired away at no trespassing signs. It was not all that unusual to hear about a deer hunter being accidentally shot by a member of his own party. Some neophytes become so stricken with buck fever, they empty their guns on imaginary targets. During one dismal season, the pet llama of a local farmer got gunned down. The same fate often threatens tawny cattle, goats, and horses. Unfortunately, I also recall a squirrel hunting companion who one day fired at a distant whitetail doe just to prove his .22 caliber proficiency. Times haven't changed, however, because I recently met a thrill killer who boasted about the rotting pile of thirty-plus prairie dogs he left behind after a trip out west. These derelicts are by no means representative of the majority sportsmen.

Midway through college, my gun-bearing jaunts began to wane. After graduating and then entering the workforce, the call to the wild resurfaced in a much different manner. Finally having a steady income, a state-of-the-art arsenal could finally be afforded. Before long, I was again prowling the fields and forests. This time, however, I missed fewer shots and came home with the proof. My fancy 35mm Pentax SLR camera with its zoom telephoto lens put me back on target. Although the hunt now resumed in a more picture-perfect way, the last time I pulled back on a steely trigger continued to haunt me. Unable to forget that deadly night, a fatal shot in the dark resounded within my memory. Ruminated again and again, the outcome could not be forgotten.

Throughout my high school days, I often joined my friend Clyde and his dad on coon hunts. As a teenager, nothing was better than running around all nightlong with an armed cohort. Amidst the shadows and silhouettes, hunting in the dark of night almost evened the playing field for me. Better yet, only one member of the party needed to carry a gun, while the rest simply joined in the excitement of keeping up with the frenzied howling. It was Clyde's grandfather who lent us his prized Bluetick Coonhound and sent us off into the frosty midnight air. After releasing the hound, we would stand silently until the canine started yelping. With flashlights beaming all about, we then tried following the dog's signals. Usually the coon would be treed after a short chase, but every once and awhile, a ringtail managed to narrowly escape over a rocky bluff or into a hillside den. Rarely, though, did we return home empty handed.

On one incredibly cold October night, we had treaded about three hours without any sign of a carousing rascal. Shivering and frustrated, all of us were near ready to give up. At long last, the howling dog tracked down a scent and quickly treed the masked varmint. After our party crossed a harvested cornfield, crawled through a rusty barbed-wire fence, and climbed an incredibly steep hill, we then reunited with the anxious hound. Searching the branches above where the dog was circling, Clyde's flashlight eventually caught a pair of glowing eyes. Always it was Clyde or his dad who did the shooting, but on this night, Clyde's dad suddenly handed me the .22 rifle and said it was my turn. This time, I did not have my trusty shotgun to make up for any lack of accuracy. Taking hold of the gun, I peered upward to pinpoint the target. Unsure about the exact location, I concentrated on the spot where Clyde and his dad's flashlight beams converged. Raising the rifle and steadying my aim, I pulled back slowly on the trigger. As the .22 reverberated in the darkness, nothing else seemed to be happening. No stirring was occurring from above. Good grief, I had proven my lack of marksmanship once again. When I began to mention something about missing the mark, Clyde's dad corrected me and pointed overhead. Suddenly, a limp figure came crashing downward through the branches. As it hit the ground, a gruesome thud could be both heard and felt. I stood somewhat in shock as remarks about my shooting prowess were voiced by Clyde and his dad. Upon closer inspection, the critter had been nailed right below the ear by a perfect shot. Although this had been a moment of triumph, my feelings were more like that of depression. Although I had at last earned the bragging rights to fit in as a hotshot among the good ol' boys, the only thing now within my view was a motionless carcass and pool of blood. Pelted for its pelt, I had completed the execution. Somehow, it just did not seem worth it.

Never do I begrudge those who hunt. It is a longstanding tradition that is cherished by many. For me, however, hunting became my way of proving that I could join in like everyone else. In reality, my venturing about with a gun in hand was nothing more than a macho excuse for spending time outdoors and peering just a little farther into the woods. By doing so, many strange and interesting critters came into my acquaintance. Perhaps it was me who was the most unusual among them. This I cannot deny. And though I continue loaded for bear, thank goodness my ammunition and ambitions have changed.

Brave Nude World

Sometimes the extraordinary is the everyday ordinary.

When beginning college, you are pretty much nobody among nobodies. It does not take long for higher education to bring former high school hotshots down a notch. As such, college levels the playing field. Everyone starts anew from classroom to campus involvement. All those hometown labels, reputations, and prior popularity, or lack thereof, remain behind as the future now begins. How sweet it is.

Whether through wisdom, fate, or sheer luck, I landed at the perfect university. At 7500-plus students, it was big enough to offer me every opportunity and small enough that getting around never became an issue. Most of all, this scholarly institution really wanted me and even arranged funding for the majority of my stay.

In the midst of the 1970's, the concepts of diversity and affirmative action began burgeoning on American campuses. Not only did this mean reaching out to racial and ethnic groups, but it also included recruiting students with challenging physical circumstances. A lot of this stemmed from the influx of war-torn Vietnam veterans embarking on new lives. It also was a time when vocational rehabilitation began partnering with higher education. As such, campuses became more sensitive and assertive toward addressing different needs. For me, this was an entry into a brave new world and another even more revealing.

It took only a short while to discover that I was no longer the novelty as in my hometown. Two doors down and across the hall from my dorm room resided Jim, the prime-time disc jockey for the campus radio station. Totally blind and hobbled by legs that did not fully extend, Jim represented my first real acquaintance with a genuine barrier buster. Perhaps I could be the same.

Farther down the hall were burly John and smiling Dave, whose legs sported metal supports, while their arms leaned on enabling crutches. Next door to me lived formidable Igor, a barrel-chested dude, who had earned this nickname due to his uneven manner of walk. Both his knees had been blown out from years of football injuries. He seemed okay with the character label, but no one dared poke fun at this muscle-bound man with an enormous upper body and a girlfriend named Killer. Unlike disc jockey Jim, Igor was more adept at busting heads than busting barriers. I guess we each adapt according to whatever works best for us.

As for the rest of my dorm mates, there was the usual compliment of young males desperately in need of detoxification or drug rehabilitation, a gay character named Iguana, Little Mexico Joe, three students from Africa, another from Turkey, two gentle giants known as Big Stick and Chopper, bass player Whitey, several Jewish guys from Chicago, space cadet Jerry, a recluse who never left his room, a nerdy resident assistant, and, of course, the usual contingency of average Joe's. Three doors down from me, there was even a hometown kid. Nicknamed Diver, his fraternity escapades steered me clear from ever jumping on the same Greek bandwagon.

At the campus cafeteria, I sat among wheelchairs, specialized braces, prosthetic limbs, white canes, thick glasses, hearing devices, and, I suspect, several challenged students like me without the visible trappings of any obvious limitation. There were also students from all races, ethnicities, religions, and walks of life. No longer feeling like that of an outsider, this menagerie symbolized to me that despite my faded signature purple bell bottoms, a new pair of orange tennis shoes, and that one other peculiarity, I had a good chance to blend in.

It did not take long to make friends of all sizes, shapes,

and sorts. Some evolved into mentors while others served as examples on how not to succeed. There always seemed to be a good balance between the two. Most of all, there was always that chance encounter with another student reflecting the same audacity and attitude to match yours. Perhaps that is what I really liked about Fred.

Tall, lanky, and bashful, Fred was a unique guy. He frequently stuttered, had a gimpy left arm that dangled at his side, and an awkward limp. His typical attire was the run-of-the-mill flannel shirt and boot-cut Levi's. Living at the north end of the dorm hall, Fred was just another freshman greenhorn similar to me. To some, however, Fred depicted a tempting target. This especially drew the aim of a well-seasoned butthead named Rex, who majored in ridiculing anyone dubbed by him as perfectly imperfect. Sharing the same dorm, the three of us routinely crossed paths.

Always dressed in a preppy look, clean shaven, and topped off with finely groomed short hair, Rex camouflaged himself as a mild-mannered mama's boy. This guy, however, represented a pedigree party animal, jerk, and, for the most part, a bully. The term *pervert* could also be added to his resume. Fred, on the other hand, was a brilliant student, extremely timid, and a guy who just wanted to fit in. The contrasting personalities of Rex and Fred would soon set the stage for both of them to star in an intriguing turn of events.

In many ways, these two guys were complete opposites. Fred was a geeky small town character, who buried himself in his books. Deviant Rex haled from a large metro area and devoted as little time as he could to academics. In his crusade to become the "Big Man on Campus," Rex deemed it necessary for students like Fred to serve as the butt of his jokes. The upperclassman status of Rex made him quite influential among the impressionable frosh. He designated himself as the dorm's main instigator and organizer of mayhem. Because of Fred's shyness and desire to fit in, Rex took it upon himself to serve as

Fred's social mentor, which, in reality, was nothing more than a sinister guise for selecting sacrificial victims.

When the spring season arrived during the second semester, Rex became infatuated with the popular streaking craze of the mid 1970's. College campuses became hotbeds for this au natural epidemic. At this time, there was even a national hit song on the charts called "The Streak." This novelty tune by Ray Stevens topped the Billboard Hot 100, reached no. 3 on the Billboard country singles, and landed at no. 1 on the international UK singles chart. According to Rex's perverted pea brain, this flashing phenomenon meant showcasing himself to an adoring audience. He thus began streaking weekly with different groups. As the semester progressed, so did his bare-it-all obsession. Rex even sprinted solo through the student union and one of the campus cafeterias. This derelict never suffered from an identity crisis and relished his role as the "Baron of the Buff." It became a personal quest by Rex to convert as many followers as possible. Topping his recruitment list was Fred.

Initially, Rex failed at persuading Fred to accompany the routine campus romps. Over and over again, he badgered Fred to join in. Finally, there came one of those warm spring nights, enticing even the best of scholars to abandon studies and throw caution to the wind. Rex convinced Fred that a select group from the dorm was embarking on a sensational streak, which he dim-wittedly christened as "bares out of hibernation." For solidarity and fellowship, Fred was needed as an honoree in this privileged pursuit. To calm any fears and uneasiness, Rex shared with Fred the master plan. Everyone was to proceed across the campus wearing only a towel. Upon Rex's command, all would hurl their towels and dash madly past the women's dorms. As a result, there would be a female chorus of cheers like never heard before at this university. Hysterical gals would even toss seductive souvenirs out of their windows. With a gift for gab, Rex made it sound all too enchanting for Fred.

Although reluctant, Fred finally conceded. In short order,

he soon found himself assembled behind his White Hall dorm and among a spirited towel-clad congregation. With Rex in the lead, this semibuff brigade marched boldly onward. Jeers and taunts could already be heard coming from the nearby women's dorms. Upon reaching the first campus residence, Rex stopped and issued final instructions to the group. Following his count to three, all towels would go airborne. The countdown then ensued. To add drama, Rex hesitated momentarily after calling out "one" and then "two." When Rex shouted three, towels shot skyward as the chaotic mob bolted forward. Fred did likewise, only to discover he had now become the exposed butt of Rex's latest joke. Rex had secretly advised everyone, except Fred, to wear gym shorts under their towels. Amidst the hysterical laughter that now erupted around him, Fred streaked awkwardly back to retrieve his towel. Embarrassed and fuming, he made a solo retreat to the dorm. Now an angry "bare," this was a setup he would never forgive or forget.

Despite being a full-fledged bonehead, Rex had his share of imitators. About a week later, one sorry copycat attempted his own lone streak across campus. Once the exhibitionist got spotted, a frenzied gang of students began chasing him. After running several blocks for his life, this desperate soul finally escaped the malicious pursuit. His effort to show-off had turned into an unforeseen showdown of nearly being skinned alive. How he ever made it back to his starting point remained unknown.

As the semester ended and finals week began, Rex concentrated on streaking instead of studying. He arrogantly strutted about one evening, announcing his intention to embark on another flash dash across campus. Although Rex tried convincing others to join him, no one responded. Undaunted, Rex proceeded with his solitary promenade. About twenty minutes later, frantic screams were suddenly heard outside the dorm. Looking out my window, I saw a birthday-suited figure pounding frantically on the glass entryway doors and cursing the locks. Although the hollering face remained in-discernible to me, the voice sounded a lot like that of Rex screaming obscenities.

Out of curiosity, I decided to take a closer look and see if anyone was bothering to respond. Midway down the hall, I encountered Fred coming from the direction of the main dorm entrance. I asked Fred if he knew that Rex was trapped outside in the nude. Fred just smirked and innocently mentioned that someone, apparently, must have locked the front doors earlier than usual. Just at that moment, an echoing police siren caught our attention. Through the hallway windows, we then noticed the rotating red lights of an approaching squad car. As the two of us walked away, I joked to Fred, "Looks like Rex's streak has finally ended." Fred then snidely exclaimed, "Ain't that the naked truth!"

When our sophomore year began, Rex was nowhere to be found. Meanwhile, revered as a campus folk hero of sorts, Fred continued his sly and scholarly ways. No doubt about it, this guy could truly grin and "bare" it. Thanks to Fred, many of us gleaned some knowledge well beyond our academic ambitions. We learned to view Fred as a friend and ally rather than an aberration. Most of all, a valuable lesson had been taught on what goes around, comes around. That's especially true no matter whether it be a brave new world or brave nude world. Without a doubt, my college experiences included both.

Treasure Islander

Seek and ye shall find. Give it the run around and you'll discover even more.

Some call it the oldest profession on earth. No, I do not mean that discreet and despicable endeavor. What I am referring to is that other form of desperation. It is the one which many of us have come to begrudge as "looking for work." After years of classroom servitude and with a university degree finally in hand, I was about to learn what this truly means. The formal lessons had ended, and my real-world education would now begin.

Upon graduating college in the late 1970's, I was more than ready to take on the world. Unfortunately, the world did not seem as ready for me or equipped for the multitudes now saturating the job-hunting market. The entire economy was on the skids. To exemplify how truly tough these times were, a drawing was held on my campus just to get an interview with the McDonald's management recruiter. No kidding, that's what really happened, and I missed out on this highly sought-after burgerland lottery. As an additional hurdle, I, of course, had to defer from any opportunities that required driving or a certain level of acuity. This ruled out the on-campus interviews for traveling sales jobs with Xerox, S.C. Johnson, IBM, and Procter & Gamble. Therefore, the meager help-wanted ads became my home base for resume submissions and rejections.

With the dismal job market overflowing with recent grads and returning Vietnam veterans, it became a competition to take whatever you could get. Reluctantly and humbly, I did just that by accepting a management trainee position with

F. W. Woolworth's. As a result, I found myself ungraciously learning the ropes of the modest five and dime trade.

Believe me, this was not the prestigious and lucrative career I had envisioned. Rather than instantly stepping into middle or upper management, I was brought back down to earth with an entry-level start. Now mired in overseeing household goods, draperies, sewing notions, music, hardware, and pet supply sections, I would have to work my way up to supervise the toy, beauty aids, confectionary, stationary, and apparel departments.

Surprisingly, everything I learned from my marketing, consumer behavior, human resources, and accounting courses would now have merit. However, the weekly schedules with added evenings, weekends, and occasional twelve hour shifts, wore me down. My life became one of all work and no play. Because of relocation, I felt marooned in a new city and state. That nearby circle of friends no longer existed. My main outlet for social activity was walking numerous blocks to the grocery store and juggling several overloaded bags on the way back.

Located in Rochester, Minnesota, the Woolworth's store I helped to manage represented your typical low-end merchandiser. Somewhat unusual for this pioneer retailer, the store anchored a major regional mall. Down one aisle, Barbie Dolls, Hot Wheels, Lincoln Logs, and Tinker toys overloaded the shelves. Along the other aisles, thumb tacks, bobby pins, magic markers, candles, kitchenware, hardware, picture frames, clothes hangers, moth balls, and brand-name remedies lay in waiting. The clothing section modeled an undergarment display, which I wanted no association with. Centered in the back, a sewing and crafts niche greeted the homemakers. The far corner hosted bird cages and a sea of smelly fish tanks that bordered the pet supplies. Near the side checkout sat racks of romance paperbacks, batteries, alphabetized record albums, obsolete eight-tracks, and the new fangled cassettes.

Showcased in the center corridor were specialty sales on

exotic houseplants, one-dollar records, seasonal decorations, discounted T-shirts, and the most recent gizmos and gadgets from TV ads. I would be remiss not to also mention the giant baskets of tacky plastic flowers, which constantly needed restocking. Next to the two front checkout registers stood several gumball machines and a curtained booth for instant photos. And because of its corner location, three huge store windows faced the Apache Mall's main walkway. It became one of my primary duties to set up promotions in each of these glassed-in stages. My Teddy Bear Tea Party and diabolical Halloween displays became pinnacles of my dime-store career.

Just inside the store entrance and governed meticulously by a gray-haired commandant, was a confectionary island of bulk Brach's candies and Planters nuts. Showcased in one bin after another were jelly beans, gumdrops, chocolate stars, malted milk balls, mints, lemon drops, cashews and roasted Spanish peanuts. And for those weary shoppers needing to sit down and refuel, an in-house diner of green vinyl booths, chrome-accented counter, and swiveling stools, offered the signature burger and fries combo. Of course, this menu always came drenched in complimentary grease and accompanied by an ice-cold soda in a genuine Coca-Cola glass.

As mundane as the merchandise often made this workplace, it did have its moments, one of which almost led to a crime scene investigation. Following a day off, I returned to work early the next morning and began organizing the premises before the arrival of the staff. At the rear of this sizable store was a huge warehouse. Within this dimly lit storage area, a small room with sliding doors at each end served as the trash depository. The trash removal company had access from the outside, while our employees could enter from the inside. Noticing that a couple of boxes with packing materials had been left out from the day before, I grabbed them and headed for this trash room. Unlocking the sliding door, I gave it a yank and simultaneously tossed the boxes through the opening. Before they even landed among the other garbage, my heart momentarily stuttered, when I caught a glimpse of what appeared to be, a naked body laying face down in the trash.

As an instinctive reaction, I slammed the door shut. While somewhat in shock, my scrambled thought process debated between calling 911 immediately or just waiting until other employees arrived. However, catching a glimpse does not generally take in all the details. What I really needed to do now required reopening that door and confirming the horrific sight. As the door slowly slid to my left, I agonized as to whether this was truly a corpse and worse yet, could it be someone I know? Not being an eagle eye by any stretch of the imagination, I needed a point-blank close-up. Therefore, I held my breath and carefully leaned forward to examine this unsettling stiff. My heart was now beating so vigorously, the pounding echoed in both ears. As I reluctantly touched the exposed right leg, its cold surface and state of rigor mortis, confirmed everything about this gruesome situation. The appendage constituted deceased plastic. Someone had tossed away one of our lifelike mannequins. Enough said about my keen observation skills. Chalk this up as just another episode of the naked truth.

Speaking of acuity, the issues involving my unique eyes, was never discussed with any of the store's employees. This included my boss and the senior assistant managers. Feeling the need to leave well enough alone, I was not motivated to bring up the subject. However, one clerk consistently went out of her way to remind me that I needed glasses, whenever she observed me operating the pricing machine. A few co-workers also kidded me about being too cheap to buy a car. All that really mattered was making it to work each day and getting the job done.

Despite an incredible Woolworth's boss and valuable training, the routine drudgery and a yearning for something more, led to my departure just over a year later. I was ready to move on, move up, and, most of all, move closer to where my fiancé lived. This meant a return to my home state of Wisconsin, where the job prospects continued to falter.

Facing the dismal daily task of scrutinizing the help-wanted ads and routinely mailing out resumes, I regressed back into familiar territory. At this pivotal point in my life, the interviews and opportunities were far and few between. The waiting game and disappointments created too much downtime and despair. Beleaguered by this dilemma, dire actions then beckoned. In a panicked mode to accomplish at least something constructive, a gut-wrenching decision was confronted. Should I rummage or run? I brazenly opted for both as a combined vocation. In doing so, I thus became a rummage runner by jogging to and fro among the weekly garage sales.

Downtime can be downright depressing. You cannot spend all your time searching for jobs and analyzing rejection letters. A healthy respite is required to rejuvenate the ambitions and detour the anxieties. If you do not choose wisely, you may be doomed to a destiny of not only religiously watching the dreary soap operas, but also becoming one yourself. The only surefire cure is to get out and about. With this goal in mind, I improvised as always.

Both rummaging and fun running were growing trends at this time. Each represented an addiction, to which I overdosed. My parents operated an antique business that eventually drew me into scavenging estate sales, flea markets, auctions, and treasure-laden garages. As for the recreational running, this simply rekindled a passion from my track days. Not willing to sacrifice either pursuit, I instead meshed together these forces.

Bear in mind, making this decision was by no means a simple ordeal. Both rummaging and running are fine arts requiring discipline and practice. They are also endeavors, which, in my situation, represented hurdles. Most rummage addicts simply scan the classifieds and then begin driving about. Not only was I unable to drive, but it also required a fairly powerful magnifier just to read the ads and city map. Afterwards, I would then plot a somewhat circular route to the nearest sales and back. Because reading signs from a distance was not an option for me, I took advantage of this small town labeling its north/south roadways as avenues and east/west corridors as streets. Once bearings were established, I then began counting the blocks while venturing onward. If by chance a wrong turn put me off course, I either relied on my memory until I found a familiar street or, in the worst-case scenario, got up as close as I could to decipher the nearest sign. If all else failed, I would forego humility and ask for directions, even if that meant I was unknowingly on 22nd St. and inquiring on how to get to 23rd St. Mind you, serious bargain hunting always supersedes humility, which segues into my next challenge.

These rambling expeditions represented encounters with anything from mounted mooseheads to dress forms, teddy bears, goofy hats, spare tires, and abandoned bowling balls. Although I had my ophthalmological limitations, I could see well enough to trek from sale to sale and spot items of specific interest. When it came to the labeled prices, this, however, was an obstacle. Some were simply in-discernible for my faulty headlights. To compensate, I turned to bargaining skills and the practice of obnoxiously asking, "What's the best you can do on this?" Rather than bending over and pressing my face to the price tags, this method seemed less contentious. Fearing the label of becoming the town's marauding Mr. Magoo, my acuity did not need to become a subject of inquisition during these searches. I also scorned the constant enlightenment of being advised, "You really need glasses." Sometimes you just grow weary of articulating about a predicament that is not easily understood. Trying to educate those around me about what I could do with my peripheral as opposed to my obscured central vision required more than a mere lecture. From my experiences, forthright explanations only confused and caused misconceptions, suspicions, and the routine commentary "But you seem so normal!".

On occasion, approaching these sales sometimes resulted in "dime-store flashbacks." Many of the items crowded on the tables conjured up reminders of Woolworth's center aisles. Once part of consumer frenzies, these trendy PrestoBurgers, FryBabies, SaladShooters, Mince-O-Matics, and Chia Pets had now lost their pizzazz. Abandoned alongside the donut makers, food dehydrators, juicers, lava lamps, pizza ovens, bread machines, and exercise equipment, these cast-offs were now relegated to give-away prices. However, scrounge further and even greater gems will be found.

Not only did this exercise of rummage running improve my physical condition, but it also became lucrative as well. Rummaging is modern-day piracy, racing from one treasure isle to the next and then figuratively stealing away all precious booty at a bargain price. After learning how to restore and refinish my discovered antiques, many of them got resold for a tidy profit. However, I spent far too much time around pungent paint stripping chemicals and fumes. Still, the rewards always seemed worth the efforts as the old lead paint melted away to then reveal the rich wood grains beneath it. This always served as a grand finale to the treasure hunts. Recreating such beautiful things is just another form of artistry.

As luck would have it, on one particular outing, I struck the mother lode of sales. The old geezer hosting this sale decided to get rid of most everything he owned. Instead of pricing the individual items, he was open to any reasonable offer. Overflowing from the garage and sprawled about his lawn were oil lamps, kerosene lanterns, tin toys, bentwood rockers, caned chairs, crocks, jugs, cast-iron kettles, and more tools than I had ever seen before. Feeling greedy, I wanted almost everything, in sight but realized that my take was limited to a two-armed carrying capacity.

One of my favorite things to collect at this time included old fishing gear, and this house-emptying elder had it all. Without hesitation, I first grabbed an iron bait casting rod. My next move involved snatching a split-bamboo fly rod, an antique willow creel, and a vintage wood-framed trout net. I completed my scavenging by nabbing a tackle box crammed with collector's lures including Jitterbugs, Hula Poppers, Creek Chubs, Suicks, and bucktail spinners. When offered a stingy ten bucks for the entire collection, the proprietor hemmed and hawed a bit before finally giving in. Also among his belongings was a rusty handcart, which I spotted just before departing. On impulse, I offered him one dollar for it and ended up with another treasure. Overloaded, I then strutted toward home.

Dangling on the left shoulder hung both the creel and trout net. In my right hand were clutched the fishing rods and tackle box. I then grabbed onto the handcart with my left hand and pulled it behind me. Walking briskly and feeling quite savvy about the booty now in my possession, I was within three blocks of home when a car pulled up alongside me. Startled somewhat, I paused as the driver began rolling down his window and leaning out through the opening. Staring me down intently, I was not sure whether this gawker was about to rob me or make an offer for my collection. With exhilaration he finally broke the silence by hollering, "Man oh man, I don't know where you're headed fishing, but I'd sure like to see what you come back with."

As this joker drove away laughing, I began wondering as to whether my rummaging around as a treasure islander was actually that great of an idea after all. Perhaps what I really needed to do is just get a job. Then again, now being so well-equipped, I might just as well go fishing instead.

Greater
Expectations

When it becomes difficult to fit in, you then fit out by outmaneuvering the obstacles and taking some outright chances.

H aving greater expectations often leads to rude awakenings. After believing that I had left the retail trade behind and was destined for bigger and better rewards, fate said otherwise. With the economy still on the skids and my prospects slim to none, I reentered the retail trade in order to make ends meet. I tried convincing myself that this new venture would be different and unique. It represented a wholesale/retail operation involving a showroom, huge warehouse, and significant catalog sales. From years of past success, it now projected future expansion to other locations. The general manager, who hired me, indicated that I would be trained at the existing locale and then promoted to take over a new showroom being planned for another city. This time I would be dealing in upper-end merchandise such as pricey camera equipment, diamond and gold jewelry, high-tech electronics, silver settings, heirloom clocks, and top of the line sporting goods. At this stage of my career, it seemed as if the clouds were now clearing, and sunnier days lay ahead. Best of all, no chance existed this time around for mannequin malarkey and trash room surprises.

During the first year of this second stint in retail management, nothing seemed to be happening. Aside from showing up each morning and locking the doors at the end of the day, I honestly cannot recall doing much else. The two other longtime managers took care of the day to day operations, while I primarily paced the showroom floor or just stood around observing the clerks and customers. Boredom evolved into a daily eight a.m. to six p.m. endurance sport.

When my second year of these doldrums began, so did some major changes. When the corporate head honcho came to town and took the management staff to Burger King for a business lunch, I suspected something was awry. It served as a Whopper revelation. Several weeks later, everyone at this store got caught off guard by the sudden announcement that longtime senior manager Richard, had been released. Although the details were vague, the corporate office simply noted that this locale could no longer afford three management staff. At the time, it seemed to me that I would be the odd man out, but instead, a very likeable and hardworking stalwart was let go. At first I sensed some resentment because fellow co-workers thought that this popular supervisor had gotten the axe in lieu of me. However, that did not matter for long, when just a few months later, all of us received notices that our jobs were being liquidated. As for my own reaction, this brought relief of sorts. With the advent of the big box stores, this place had become a dying breed. As such, I desperately needed to seek an opportunity with more potential to flourish in the long run.

In the months that followed, I found good fortune in bits and pieces. During the process of searching for a new full-time position, my employment instead culminated into four part-time jobs. Throughout the week, I managed the student union at a local state university. On weekends, my role turned to crooner and guitarist as the house entertainer at a private club. Under the stage name Critter, I also performed from time to time at area folk festivals. Between all this, a small upstart advertising agency hired me to design and market promotions for its tourism guidebook. And because all of these ventures still didn't seem to be enough, I also created my own mail-order sporting goods business. Called the Wind River Workshop, this not-so-enterprising undertaking ended up a tedious breakeven experiment.

Sometimes fate steps in when you least expect it. Unbeknownst to me, a regular patron of the private club, where I performed my musical sets, included the district administrator for a regional healthcare corporation. It just so happened that his company was the same one currently employing my wife as a social services director. Coincidentally, this administrator's wife had been a loyal customer of the showroom I used to manage. Therefore, I had a chance connection to both parties. Due to their collaboration and awareness of my present situation, an offer got extended to train me as a healthcare administrator. Sounding both challenging and well paid, I immediately accepted this opportunity with few questions asked. Shortly thereafter, the packing began for my relocation to a neighboring state. If not for financial and full-time employment needs, I perhaps should have been less anxious and more inquisitive about this career leap. Nonetheless, I once again headed westward to Southern Minnesota.

Lacking a health-care background and any significant exposure to long term care centers, I now found myself in charge of a hundred-plus staff at a 136-bed facility. To assist my acclimation to this new field, I was assigned the former facility administrator as my preceptor. This was to continue until I completed all state administrator licensure requirements. My preceptor had been promoted to a larger facility in a nearby town and was highly regarded by my direct supervisor, the district administrator.

Less than two weeks into this administrator job, unforeseen disaster struck. Although my wife and I had moved most of our belongings into a new residence, Dianna remained back at our old apartment to finish out her workplace commitments. When she phoned me at my office, I could already sense something had gone terribly wrong. Dianna had just returned from the hospital emergency room, where it was confirmed that our twins were lost because of a miscarriage. Our anticipated family factored heavily into the decision to start this new career of mine. What bothered me most of all, however, was being marooned here at my new job and unable to race back to Dianna. Although I had learned to adapt to life without wheels, this time the distance and my faulty headlights, combined for a dismal reality check.

Even though I was not the most experienced of managers, it did not take long to discover the red flags at this new work environment. During my first meeting with the chatty longtime director of housekeeping, her feedback included a comment that I was the youngest of the administrators she had worked for at this place. When I asked how many that represented, this upper middle-aged lady with graying hair began to count her fingers. After adding up the toll, her surprising answer was nine over the last eleven years. This, of course, meant that administrators either flew the coop almost yearly, or promotions were fast and furious.

From the very beginning, the district administrator and I were on uneasy terms. Occurring daily, he contacted me in regard to patient census. Some days I even received multiple calls. The body count loomed crucial at this proprietary operation. Whatever it takes, keep the beds filled. There existed an extreme pressure to admit and delay the discharge of any and all patients. Little or no scrutiny should warrant as to whether they needed to be here or not.

Because this particular facility lacked a waiting list, my boss always went ballistic whenever the patient count declined. As an irony, this situation was completely the opposite of what Dianna experienced in her previous social services position. Although owned by the same company, the center where she worked maintained two waiting lists, one for private pay and the other for Medicaid patients. In this circumstance, she got directed to disregard fair play and favor the private pay applicants over those on public assistance. Eventually, this admissions duty was taken away from Dianna for not practicing this preference. The person responsible for stripping her of admissions management was none other than my current boss.

It did not take long for me to learn about other mandates by this supervisor. In the event of a patient being discharged or passing away on any given day, strict instructions called for immediate staff reductions to the minimal level allowed by state regulations. This penny-pinching measure inflamed the ire of the representative labor union and led to numerous employee disputes. The accounting system was so miserly that even the routine cost for coffee consumed by the patients was monitored. The bottom line demanded maximized resident stays with minimized care costs. Once again and above all, do whatever it takes to keep the beds filled in this home sweet home.

To deal with the district administrator, I often sought the advice of my counterparts at other facilities within this corporation. Their counseling became like a tug-of-war, with half seeking a vendetta against this guy and the others living in fear of him. To call his reputation fiercely notorious would be a gross understatement. At one point, this belligerent overseer commented to me that never would he allow himself to spend his remaining days in one of these care centers. He truly meant it and seemed to despise the very business under his command. His wife, who also ran one of the facilities in this company, shared a similar notoriety.

It did not take long to realize the measures being taken to meet the profit-making mandates. During a facility inspection with my boss, I pointed out the shabby nature of furniture in one of the rooms. The veneer was both peeling off and partially removed from a chest of drawers. The bedding was extremely faded and on the verge of becoming threadbare in spots. The ragged curtains matched them in character and condition. A number of floor tiles had sustained cracks. Even the limited acuity of my faulty headlights could readily discern all this. As a solution, he suggested this room be reserved for patients less aware of their surroundings, such as those who were visually impaired or afflicted with dementia. From both a professional and personal standpoint, this really ticked me off. Furthermore, the room now in question was by no means an exception.

This unique care center represented an aristocratic old mansion. Converted to a nursing home, the original building housed intermediate care wards with skilled care wings added on to it. While maintaining its vintage charm, parts of this place often needed more physical therapy than the patients themselves. Several of the multiple bed wards and communal bathrooms resembled a mid-twentieth century infirmary. In contrast, my immense office, showcasing French doors and a fireplace, was larger than some of the patient rooms. Because of the three steps leading into this office, none of the patients with wheelchairs or walkers could access this area.

As an interesting irony, the male social worker in charge of admissions at this facility just happened to be married to the social worker at the nearby competing, nonprofit care center, which boasted a lengthy waiting list. It was a common practice for the wife of my facility's social worker to contact him in order to refer cast-off and less desirable patients who had extensive care needs. Wanting to move into administrator ranks and knowing that filling beds was the utmost priority, my social worker did whatever possible to score points with upper management. This again included favoring admission of private pay over Medicaid patients, a ratio requiring daily reporting as well.

To explain this not-so-merry-go-round of admissions, state laws at this time allowed long term care facilities to charge private pay patients a rate considerably higher than that for public assistance patients. Putting it bluntly, the private payees represented the greater profits. Therefore, no matter how long a Medicaid individual had been on any waiting list, the incentive was to bump that person in favor of a more lucrative bedwarmer. Therefore, this encouraged a discriminatory system, whereby money counted more than care needs.

Perhaps I was too green and oversensitive, but it appeared to me that some of the patients did not belong in this environment. With home health care and group homes not readily available, many of these patients had become institutionalized due to a primary diagnosis of developmental disability, blindness, or hearing loss. Sometimes it was even mobility that led to placement here. This got exemplified for me by Duane, a guy not much older than me, who lived in a dimly lit room on the second floor. Because of muscular dystrophy, far too much of his life seemed confined to a wheelchair and distanced from any peers. There was no doubt that he was visibly disabled, still it always bothered me how this young man in the early stages of his life, appeared marooned here among elders in their twilight years. It scared the heck out of me when pondering where I could end up some day, should my faulty headlights go out completely and other health problems surface. Would the shabby room with the beat-up furnishings be reserved for me?

In regard to Duane, you could not help but notice the Minnesota Vikings football posters plastered about his dreary room. It just so happened that shortly after meeting this patient, I participated in a community fun run. One of the celebrities helping to promote this event was defensive end, Allen Page, a member of the Vikings' famous Purple People Eaters. While jogging alongside Mr. Page, I mentioned Duane and somehow managed to entice the football legend to personally visit this devoted fan of his. Following the 5K run, Mr. Page did just that and created a lifetime memory for everyone involved. It became the most light that ever shined in Duane's room. Once again, my running paid dividends.

Dumbfounded by this corporate practice of stockpiling patients, I was gullible enough to believe that the true rewards related to this job would come from the care and comfort of elders, rather than the financial benefits created by their miseries. To deal with the situation, delusions of grandeur surfaced. If possible, I would become a reformer and change all this. Being a neophyte, I just failed to foresee how being both an advocate and administrator could result in anything but a healthy combination. At this time, I really needed to heed the advice of a former mentor, who always reminded me "never attempt to be holier than the pope."

Primary to my job was the routine accounting of revenues and expenses. As I began auditing the books, it became quite evident how my predecessor managed to keep costs down. Left behind was a myriad of festering unpaid bills, which now showed up on my balance sheet. As the new kid on the block, I lacked any leverage in discussing this concern with upper management. My preceptor, who had left behind these debts, turned the tables by claiming that I failed to understand the management of payables and receivables.

Intensifying these woes, the ongoing history of labor disputes between this employer and the local union quickly revealed itself. My district supervisor absolutely reviled unions and often forwarded taunting letters to the union leaders. However, when he began insisting that my signature appear on his scripted tirades, I knew this meant trouble. The more questions I raised, the deeper I entered into the doghouse. My director of nursing further fueled the labor union animosity by driving across town one day and somehow gaining access to the apartment of a nurse's aide. Convinced that the employee was faking illness by not reporting to work, this nursing supervisor allegedly entered the employee's bedroom to awaken her with threatening demands that she come to work. Because this nursing supervisor was married to one of the big wigs in this small town, my boss insisted that her actions be fully supported. In response, the union filed charges of trespassing and harassment in this case.

Most large companies engender a corporate culture, and

this enterprise was no exception. Each year, all administrators, along with their spouses, gathered together for the regional summer conference and administrators golf outing. Participation was not an option, even for individuals, who, such as me, had never teed off. Everyone was required to get into the swing of things. Before the day ended, I not only learned all about golf course hazards, but also actually became one. Due to my unique acuity, I relied on Dianna's assistance to locate the putting greens and track down errant drives. This was like the déjà vu of once again hunting about with my shotgun. I just aimed in a general direction and fired away. As for my ricocheted shot off the district administrator's cart, that was purely an accident. The tally of my golf game strokes would have resulted in a major stroke for most golfers.

Adding to the audacious work environment, the corporation which owned this healthcare facility suddenly merged with a larger and even more profit-hungry conglomerate. Dissention within the ranks rapidly ensued. The resulting fallout of the more experienced administrators was obvious as they jumped ship to pursue other opportunities. However, this exodus then created a management opening located closer to my hometown and family. After indicating my interest and receiving feedback from the district administrator, arrangements were made for me to visit the facility and meet the staff.

Shortly after returning from my trip, I met with my boss to discuss this opportunity. Just as our meeting ended, my boss caught me off guard by inquiring as to why my wife chauffeured me to this facility visit. Although I first noted it was important for her to see this area and confer on any mutual decision to move, I nervously added that I do not drive. In this Magoo moment, I then tried to explain the reasons for not having a driver's license and assure how my situation is adequately accommodated. Up to this point, never had I missed a day of work or any outside meetings and training sessions. How I arranged to do so seemed like no one's business but mine. Furthermore, it had not mattered in my previous jobs. Despite this reality and my current job not requiring a drivers' license or routine driving, I now sensed the ominous scrutiny of this supervisor.

Less than two weeks later, the district administrator contacted me with a frantic concern that my administrative licensure had yet to be finalized. In response, I noted that completion of all requirements were actually ahead of schedule and well within the state's interim timeframe. Nonetheless, my boss continued ranting over the licensure process. Although I offered to contact the state licensure board for confirmation, my supervisor declined any remedy. Instead, he insisted on remaining obsessed and possessed over this issue. He then changed the direction of the conversation with a perplexing twist. Starting the following week, I would begin orienting a new administrator, hired recently by the corporate office. Surprisingly, this new hire was not unfamiliar to me. As the former administrator of a nearby facility, he had suddenly departed his position following the uproar and fallout caused by a heated employee strike. Knowing the district administrator's deep-rooted hatred for organized labor, it almost seemed like this new hire came as spite toward the local union. Gullibly, I considered this grooming of another administrator, as the needed replacement for my anticipated transfer.

Exasperating the situation even more so, were the undermining antics of my social worker, who often called and complained to upper management whenever he disagreed with any of my practices or opinions. Because of what appeared to be his lack of backbone in advocating for the patients, my wife nicknamed this guy "Worm." He continually reeled over the fact that I got the head honcho position instead of him. To further complicate matters, tensions had intensified between us, following my discovery of an open bottle of liquor in his office. He needed that bottle more than ever upon learning of being passed over again, as an additional administrator was now coming on board.

To say the very least, this place was in a mess. I had come to learn the reasons for its rampant turnover of administrators. A number of its patients were simply waiting to transfer to another facility. Many of the staff wanted to do likewise. Quite frankly, it was the most downtrodden and least reputable among the four long term care centers in this small Minnesota town. Overbuilt in terms of demand, in no way could this community support so many facilities. Without a doubt, I readily awaited the chance to turn over the reins and transfer back to my home state.

While initiating orientation with this new arrival, my future status remained unclear. One week later, the district administrator informed me that my anticipated transfer could not be worked out, and because there were now two administrators at this facility, I would be the odd man out. Provided with a severance package, the circumstance then got portrayed as an indeterminate layoff until further management openings occurred. Although perplexing, drawing conclusions about this action was not all that difficult. Only weeks before, I was considered for a transfer, shortly afterward, I then noted a vision condition unrelated to work performance, and, in sequence, became discarded. So was this exit due to my limited acuity or rather a limited tolerance of the events around me? Probably, it stemmed from both faulty headlights and a naïve tendency to step too often on the brakes over ethical issues. As consolation, my replacement lasted only a matter of months.

Within the next year, I completed licensure and accepted an assistant administrator position at a newly opened nonprofit facility in Minneapolis. This Catholic affiliated organization was a complete opposite of the proprietary environment I had previously experienced. In comparison, it seemed overstaffed, over-budgeted, and overzealous in its operations. In this brand spanking new facility, my boss was a Franciscan nun with a recent entry into healthcare management. Soon I would learn how good intentions do not always translate into good business.

Just as I stepped into the promises of this new opportunity, disaster struck once again. Four days into my new position, the Mayo Clinic contacted me with an emergency call. While waiting for her scheduled GI exam, Dianna unexpectedly collapsed at this renowned clinic. Although there could be no better place for immediate attention, she was rushed to surgery and remained hospitalized for five weeks. Like the start of my last job, this became a trying time for the two of us. Never before had I experienced someone so close to me suffering such extreme pain. After a difficult recovery, Dianna returned home weighing less than eighty pounds and appearing as if she had been recently released from some dreadful refugee camp. Now living within a major metropolitan area and relocated even farther away from our families, the challenges were the greatest that we had ever faced. To counter the enormous stress, we resorted to the impulsive act of getting a Samoyed puppy. It is incredible how a little furball can soften rough times. That is what Misty did for us. However, her teething on the furniture and the hole in the carpet were absolutely unnecessary.

At the time of my arrival, this unique and long anticipated center already had a patient waiting list exceeding well over one hundred. Hyped as a Shangri-La for ailing seniors, everyone in the surrounding community wanted dibs on this place for their aging loved ones. Sometimes these demands turned political as potential patients and their families finagled to move up the long list. Although publicly funded, I often bit my lip when hearing how placement decisions were influenced by one's church affiliation. That is what happens when two Catholic priests maintain membership on your board of directors. On the other hand, the former city mayor presided as president of this board and seemed to be repaying past favors through the selective admission process. Oddly enough, even the local mortician also participated on this board.

The design of this intermediate and skilled care facility was immaculate, but not necessarily practical nor strictly adhering to the overwhelming regulations of this business. I still remember my first day when touring the facility and passing a room where construction noise could be heard. When I inquired as to whether this was a staff remodeling project in progress, my boss replied that John, who now resided in this room, had brought in his personal arsenal of power tools to make a few changes. I then cringed at the thought of liability and building code compliance.

Kitchenettes had been installed at the end of the hallways so that any patient could prepare a meal. As a result, burning food and fire alarms became a way of life until the state inspectors stepped in. Leftovers stored indefinitely in the refrigerators also became a bone of contention. To further enhance a homey ambiance, fine furniture had been purchased rather than the traditional commercial grade. In just the first year of operation, splintered armrests and snapped spindles took its toll on the comfy wooden glider rockers. All the cushioned dining room chairs required reupholstering with plastic covers, as did the entryway and rest-area furnishings. The artistic decorations and pictures placed throughout the hallways soon began disappearing. The priests and nuns associated with this center refused to accept the reality that thievery could exist in such a sacred setting.

The facility's unique architecture involved the construction of a 150-bed, three level unit attached to both a dormant parochial school and still active community church. The newly built entryway, which directly connected the care center to the quaint old church, became an ongoing escape route for wayfaring patients. Whether it was from full-blown dementia or mild confusion, patients of this nature would proceed into the church from this side entry and later exit through the back door. By the time our panicked staff caught up with them, these longtime parishioners were heading home in the same manner as they had habitually done for so many prior years.

Mimicking the patient admissions process, the selection of staff often got based on religious affiliation. Working at this fanciful and faith-based center was coveted by the loyal parishioners living in the nearby neighborhoods. The hurried pace to get this place operating, resulted in an abbreviated screening of background and reference checks. This, however, quickly took its toll. As I anxiously dove in to assist this organization, a sixty percent turnover of staff had already transpired in its inaugural year. Work compensation claims were rocketing. Employee disputes had burgeoned. And, of course, expenses now threatened to overtake the revenues. In sacrilegious irony, it felt as if I had jumped from a hellish fire into a holy frying pan. Maybe, just maybe, I should have paid more attention to the "Welcome Dan" sign placed outside my office entrance. It was affixed to a salvaged funeral wreath on a tripod. Flowery arrangements, left behind from local funerals, routinely end up at care centers like this, which, I suppose, could symbolize a new beginning as well as a memorialized ending.

Similar in size to my last facility, whose business office assistants consisted of only one full-time and one part-time employee, this place supported an inflated administrative troupe that included three nuns, an ex-priest, a nicotine addict forever AWOL on smoke breaks, and a personnel director compulsively obsessed with psychoanalyzing employees as passive/aggressive. One of the office nuns was terminally ill with cancer and could barely make it through each day. Due to confidentiality, the extent of her illness could not be disclosed to staff. Following a reorganization of this office, her condition rapidly deteriorated. Upon her sudden passing, a rumor circulated that she succumbed from the changes recently implemented by the newcomer assistant administrator.

For varying reasons, certain staff and board members, who were attracted to this highly-touted center, appeared to have a chip on their shoulders. In some cases, it was more like a boulder. The director of social services managed to have her parents admitted as residents and then proceeded to constantly demand preferential treatment for them. This escalated into a personal vendetta. Through the assistance of an instigating board member, she accessed personnel records in a scheme to implicate any staff members adversarial to her expectations. Like a clandestine spy, this social worker routinely solicited gossip from a nosy maintenance man, who did little more than wander room to room while visiting old friends. The main criteria for hiring this custodian was that he had lived in the neighborhood all his life and occasionally cleaned the church. He also was a close ally of the parish priest, who utilized him for personal espionage.

Many of the nuns assigned as department heads were former parochial school educators. As a result, they struggled immensely with the realities and shortcomings of the healthcare system. To the ire of the staff, these nuns received extra benefits and housing. This caused a rift especially with the nurse's aides, cooks, and housekeepers, who strained to make ends meet. As an intriguing sideshow, the interactions between these good sisters oftentimes resembled sibling rivalries.

From time to time, you could sense an uneasy relationship among the staff nuns who lived together in a house next door to this center. When the boss and several subordinates interact on a twenty-four hour basis, the separation of work and home life presents an ongoing challenge. As a result, these good sisters received no daily respite from personality conflicts or job-related issues.

Behind the scenes brewed a subtle civil war. Not inclined to conceal any chauvinism, the stern and condescending parish pastor made it known that women, especially nuns, should be limited in leadership roles. As rebuttal, my Franciscan boss scorned one particular board member, whom she referred to as the pastor's houseboy. This middle-aged and unemployed man fueled many a rumor in reference to his relationship with this priest. Having little else to do, this incredibly strange man frequently skulked about the facility during all times of the day and night while giving many of us the creeps. Oftentimes, this eccentric board member joined forces with the director of social services in dredging up scuttlebutt and complaints. These two agitators even intimidated the personnel director into releasing employee files to them. It seemed like they were hoping to uncover dark secrets about co-workers. As such, this dastardly duo got access to my file, which led the director of social services to confront and criticize me for having nothing more than a background with Woolworth's. Considering the old-timer clientele of Woolworth's, I probably had a better understanding of geriatrics than this so called counseling professional, who, by the way, soon thereafter got removed from her position.

Healthcare politics do not always blend well with religious passions. As innovative as this center aspired to be, the rigidity of state regulations can butt heads with the best of ideas. It became an antagonistic ordeal when I oftentimes had to advise both my boss and the board members on regulatory realities. As an example, I was soundly chastised one day for choosing to respond to a fire alarm rather than meeting with the parish pastor. Despite attempting later to explain my licensure obligations, Father William took this as a personal insult and had no desire to absolve me after my confession of administrative responsibility. From his old-school perspective, I was first and foremost subordinate to God and him, rather than any state regulatory entity.

In what amounted to a comical payback, this clergyman later reported me for behavior related to alcohol consumption. However, this misinterpretation actually represented a situation of "doggone it." The facility had recently adopted a pet therapy dog named Brandy. Trained by the local humane society, this shaggy new resident starred as an instant hit among most everyone here. Unfortunately, a patient accidentally left an exterior door ajar during Brandy's first day. As a result, the curious canine took off to inspect the neighborhood. Somehow, it then became my responsibility to track him down. Anxious to quickly retrieve this long-eared escapee, I began searching the area and calling out, "Brandy!" Unaware of this dog and its name, the pastor heard my calls and deliberately assumed I was hunting for hooch instead of pooch. When later advised that my actions were that of a dogcatcher, this priest appeared miffed about the truth. Old-school parsons, just do not like to be corrected.

In another effort to add creature comforts, a University of Minnesota project lent its talking bird to this center. The goal of this pet therapy program involved to motivating stroke patients to regain their speech by conversing with this feathered friend. Although it was never ascertained, who was to blame, someone taught this bird several obscenities, which this critter obnoxiously repeated, over and over.

Tolerance is not always first and foremost in religious-affiliated organizations. During the annual Christmas staff party, all hell broke loose when our personnel director's daughter showed up with her date. This daughter also worked for us as a nurse's aide. Her accompanying date came leather-clad in Harley fashion and festooned with chains. To the shock of my boss, this date was not a mister but a miss instead. As soon as the couple embraced and began slow-dancing, my boss blew a fuse and demanded I do something. In sincerity, I jokingly responded that the brawny leather lady was far more muscular than me. Sister Boss was not amused.

Several weeks later, my boss approached me about another problem employee. Caught off guard, Sister wanted me to get rid of a staff member named Clarence. When asked why, she then noted that this guy had a visual impairment more extensive than realized at the time of his initial hiring. Unbeknownst to her, my eyes were not much better than those of Clarence. Fearful of the same scrutiny, I was not about to share any in-depth details of my situation, nor willing to dispose of someone in a similar circumstance. As I argued on Clarence's behalf, Sister's frustrations escalated, and my once again entry into the doghouse became obvious.

About this same time, a disturbing pattern began evolving. I fully understood the need to fire both the oft-absent, chain-smoking office worker and insurgent social worker. However, I really became upset when my boss decided to replace the maintenance and housekeeping director by stating that he simply could not keep up with the job. Afflicted with polio at a younger age, this crutch-enabled man inspired me with his attitude and abilities. In my opinion, he fell victim to the facility's design problems, due not on his part but attributed more so to the highly touted architect residing on the board of directors. The next to fall out of favor was the assistant director of nursing. Seriously injured in an auto accident and out of work for months, my boss voiced ongoing concerns about allowing this rehabilitated nurse back on staff. Perhaps what disturbed me most was the rapid exit of the young director of nursing. Shortly after the traumatic diabetes diagnosis of this department head, questions of her management skills began surfacing. A decision then quickly ensued to replace her with an older and more seasoned professional.

Although the timing may have been coincidental, my perspective on this sequence of events left me questioning the organization's humanity and conscience. My advocacy tendencies once again ignited. At a point in both her life and profession, this young director of nursing needed the support of the center and staff more than ever. As a co-worker, she had become a trusted colleague of mine. Rather than from a medical condition, her downfall was the result of an unrealistic workplace culture that viewed itself as well-meaning, yet haplessly failed to understand the physical and fiscal limitations of this business.

By no means was my boss a bad person. Her passion to make this place succeed had no parallel. Like far too many, however, she and the board members appeared to let their personal prejudice get the better of them. As this pattern persisted, portraying any kind of occupational and physical flaw, turned into a feared label of damaged goods. It is a reality in some workplaces which often panic rather than accommodate.

As previously noted, this health-care center was full of good intentions yet overloaded with start-up costs, personnel pitfalls, and a state funding system that would never match aspirations. Something had to give, and so it did. In a move to downsize and restructure, positions had to be eliminated. My vulnerable assistant capacity served as a prime target. To be quite honest, a center this size could not afford two full-time licensed administrators. As such, the board decided to whittle the two upper management slots down to one. In this transition, my boss became relegated to a new role away from day to day operations. Although I applied for the newly created lone administrator position, a candidate with a far more extensive background earned the nod. As for me, I got a going-away party, a modest severance check, and the gratuitous parting gift of an engraved clock.

My somewhat short term tenure in long term care did have an upside by creating additional credentials. Throughout this period, I became president of an American Cancer Society chapter and vice president of a community clinic, served as chairman of a state aging and wellness coalition, presented forums at several healthcare association conferences, organized a senior health fair, spearheaded an urban revitalization project, and published a nationally distributed newsletter called "*Welltrends.*" During this era, I began evolving into an overachiever. I basically felt an ongoing need to be better, just in order to be equal. Based on my personal experiences, as many plusses as possible were needed to counter that certain minus of mine.

For a time, I considered remaining in this field. Although I liked healthcare administration, the daily grind of paperwork and policy reviews was taking its toll. The headaches and fatigue from constant eyestrain forecast storms ahead if I continued driving in this same direction. Something had to change, and that, it did. My greater expectations would now take me on a different course and to a place far away. Unforeseen, I headed to a distant land of intriguing adventures and outlandish characters. And in spite of these headlights being somewhat faulty, they continued to lead me down new roads.

Throughout these early years of my work life, it never seemed necessary or wise to begin any job by emphasizing a limitation. Although I could not see well, I viewed myself as seeing well enough. Survival for me, relied on my accentuating the positive and overlooking that negative, which others found hard to understand. Some will criticize this approach and claim that the unfortunate experiences may have been avoided with an upfront revelation. Perhaps on rare occasions, this can be true. During this era of both my resume and ADA regulations still being in their formative stages, I had to contend with the reality of the times and curtail the risks. Shortly ahead however, this scenario would soon change.

Dr. Heckle and Mr. Hide

Pursuing new challenges means never leaving well enough alone.

Desperate times call for desperate measures. With my administrator position eliminated by corporate restructuring and once again facing the inevitable task of finding a new job, it was time for extremely drastic action. Because of past twists and turns, a change in direction now beckoned. As such, I searched my soul, searched the ads, and then followed that age-old sage advice to "go West, young man."

To be quite honest, the administrator job loss did not hail as a tragic episode in my career life. Despite giving it a worthy effort, I was not particularly fond of the endless regulatory rigmarole and ethical dilemmas of healthcare management. After enduring the good, the bad, and the ugly, of the long term care business, I needed a change. Worn-out by dealing with the barrage of budget and personnel issues, I just wanted a return to my marketing roots. Perhaps I could remain in the medical field and now specialize in promotions and public relations.

As the exploration into new avenues began, I deviated from my staunch resistance for any outside guidance and contacted the Minnesota Division of Vocational Rehabilitation. This was a major step for me. Even though I had always qualified for voc-rehab assistance, I stubbornly considered it a letdown to enlist any help. Fortunately, I came to my senses at a time when DVR programs were on an upswing and adequately staffed. The state's services actually had a full-time placement specialist, who suggested that I consider working for the federal government. Through what was termed a Schedule A appointment, my status allowed me to bypass civil service exams and compete for current openings. After laboring through the lengthy SF-170 application process, I started sending out resumes and forms to federal agencies all over the country. Most of these were to U.S. Department of Veteran Affairs medical centers, where I felt my past health-care administration experiences could be best utilized. To my surprise, one of the centers totally agreed and offered me an appointment as a public affairs specialist. The only catch to this endeavor, however, required that I accept a temporary one year appointment and relocate to a remote corner of civilization known as Walla Walla.

For years, I wanted to venture westward and live near the mountains. When I discovered that this place bordered the Blue Mountains and Wallowa range and also was in close proximity to the Cascades, my time had come. The small hospital and active outpatient clinic located here served a three-state region of Southeast Washington, Southwest Idaho, and Northeast Oregon. After researching this particular VA medical center, I learned that it was a historic military outpost now converted to a medical complex. From its mid-1800s cavalry start by Company E, Ninth Infantry, the mission of this old fort had gone from hoofbeats to heartbeats. Preserved on this site were the ordinance magazine, granary, ordinance storehouse, infantry barracks, gateway, chapel, stables, blacksmith shop, oil-house, commanding officer's quarters, parade grounds, and an ancient cemetery with the marked graves of soldiers and early settlers.

Along the southern boundary of this site were restored fort residences, which originally served as officers' quarters and currently housed medical center staff. Oftentimes, these vintage homes of lofty ceilings and stucco walls became recruitment perks to attract healthcare professionals to this out of the way center. Not being able to drive, access and distance to work were always a personal concern. When divulged to me that one of the residences was vacant, I negotiated with the personnel director to see if I could move in. Although he stated that the vacant residence was being held for recruitment of a long-needed urologist for the surgery program, I finally convinced him to allow me temporary use of this place until a surgeon was hired. Within the next month, my Minneapolis home got emptied into an Allied moving van and carted off to the Great Northwest.

My job as the public affairs officer involved management of public relations, marketing, and assisting with the volunteer program at this medical campus for U.S. military veterans. Even before this new role began, a huge PR issue emerged upon my arrival. Larry, the personnel director, who was big on equal employment opportunity (EEO), announced to the staff that a legally blind individual had just been hired. Although this had been done with good intentions, communications got mixed up when it was noted that I would be living in the residence being held for the urology surgeon. It did not take long for word to spread throughout this close-knit community, that a blind surgeon had been hired. Many of the veterans who relied on this center for their medical needs panicked over the prospect of an out of sight surgeon working on their vital organs. Eventually, I was able to overcome yet another Magoo moment and convinced the vets that I had no intention of operating on anyone.

For the first time in my life, I now began a career with my unique circumstances being shared within the workplace. By no means, did this transform everyone into truly understanding these faulty headlights of mine. Some considered and contemplated my situation, while many did not. There was always a question or two, confusion, and scrutiny. This became a time of learning to deal with others as they learned to deal with me.

This awkward chapter was only the beginning of my Wild-West culture shock. I had already encountered Dr. Heckle and would soon meet Mr. Hide. Less than two weeks into this new job, I looked up from my desk to see a short middle-aged man, clad in bib overalls and topped off with a weathered cowboy hat. Standing inquisitively in the doorway, he then stepped into my office and asked if I might possibly be the new guy. Following my concurrence, he then introduced himself as "Hamm" and stated that he was here on behalf of the Elks lodge. Although his name seemed somewhat odd to me, I was familiar with the Elks organization. With that, I asked Hamm what I could do for him and the Elks. He then replied, "I've got your hides." I hesitated for a minute and countered, "Let me see if I've got this right. Your name is Hamm. You are here on behalf of the Elks. And you have my hides." "That's right," Hamm noted. "Where should I put them?"

At this point, I felt absolutely sure that some kind of newcomer trick was being played on me. In the back of my mind, however, I began considering the fact that this medical center did indeed have a psychiatric ward. Somewhat cautious and deciding to play along, I joked to Hamm, "I suppose these are elk hides." Hamm didn't seem to see the humor in my remark and answered, "Of course they are." Continuing to play along, I countered again, "I guess you'll just have to show me these hides." With that challenge put forth, Hamm escorted me out to his truck, pulled back a tarp covering the truck bed, and displayed a huge pile of processed elk hides. More than befuddled, I stared at these tawny skins while taking in their strong leathery essence. Noting my confused state, Hamm then educated me how the Elks clubs in this region, work with local hunters to provide tanned elk hides for use by disabled vets in the hospital's recreational therapy program. These recovering vets then fashion the hides into belts, knife sheaths, wallets, and other leather goods.

Even though this hide-and-seek experience now made sense, I remained unsettled for quite some time. To calm my nerves, I treaded over to the office of the staff person, who had previously worked with the volunteers and service organizations.

This co-worker named Robert, listened intently as I rambled about what had just happened. When I finally finished, he smirked back at me and said, "That's really nothing. Just wait until someone from the Lions Club shows up." Startled again and not sure what else lay ahead, I stood there pondering about how wild this Wild-West once was and still is.

Over time, I would come to know how incredibly dedicated organizations such as the Elks are to helping America's veterans. Others just as committed included the American Legion, Veterans of Foreign Wars (VFW), Vietnam Veterans of America, AMVETS, Eagles, Lions, Paralyzed Veterans of America, Military Order of the Purple Heart, and RSVP. While at this particular VAMC, I saw how the Disabled American Veterans (DAV) set up an extensive van transportation network. There was even a local auxiliary which created a memorial rose garden on these grounds. Before joining the federal government, I had no idea about the hundreds of volunteers contributing thousands of hours at each VA medical center. And if not for these organizations, my job would never have existed.

Due to some federal finagling with budget cuts, a congressional proposal was made to reduce the number of VA medical centers. As a test run for this politically hot issue, the Walla Walla VA Medical Center got targeted. As a small medical complex in a remote area, knocking off this center seemed like an easy bout. This attempt, instead, rallied the troops. The area veterans and their supporting cast of civic organizations fought back to save this medical center. However, rumors of this place closing, created a public relations disaster. A public affairs specialist needed to come on board and get out the word that the storm was over. Thus, it became my job to issue the sunnier forecasts.

Working together with the volunteers and civic organizations, I soon became acquainted with both the locals and the lay of the land. Not only was this medical center unique, but the region around it also portrayed a diverse geography. To the north of Walla Walla rolls the golden wheat fields of the Palouse. South of town are the orchards and ranch lands. Directly west is a sagebrush realm referred to as the Scablands. On this desolate acreage resides the Hanford Nuclear Reservation, which produced the first atomic bomb. Finally, to the east towers the rugged terrain of the Blue Mountains, Wallowa Range, and Tiger Canyon. Within this wilderness are critters such as cougars, elk, mule deer, coyotes, bighorn sheep, and an unusual population of black bears, whose color variations include silver, cinnamon, and blonde. This remote enclave also claims numerous sightings of "bigfoot," or what the native tribes call the "Great Hairy Man." Also within this region, flow the Columbia and Snake Rivers, which served as pathways for Lewis and Clark.

Such a varied landscape transpires into an interesting cast of characters. Many of the veterans patronizing this medical center were genuine cowboys, ranchers, mountain men, and indigenous Native Americans. As a result, I got introduced to tribal councils, rodeos, cowboy poetry, salmon fishing, mountaineering, and, of course, elk hunting.

After settling in to Walla Walla, I discovered a long-lost relative. Upon being tipped off by my mother that a cousin of my grandfather resided here, I contacted Anne Marie. As a genealogy buff, she got really excited over this connection to an outstretched branch of her family tree. Anne Marie was a retired English teacher, whereas her husband, Al, served as a former superior court judge. Having travelled the world, this couple entertained Dianna and I with many stories and routine feasts. They also taught us to never underestimate any links to faraway kin.

Despite the warm and compassionate nature of Anne Marie and Al, their lives were touched by heart-wrenching episodes. Their firstborn son died in a tragic sailing accident. Adding to this crisis, the younger son got diagnosed with multiple sclerosis. As a result, this family became quite active in the MS Society. When Anne Marie and Al mentioned that the local chapter needed to come up with a fundraising venue, I had just discovered an interesting old file in my office. It showcased how the medical center used to sponsor charity bed races in years past. This quirky competition involved attaching any kind of wheels to a bed frame, next placing a mattress and rider on top of it, and then having a team of four runners push this mobile contraption over a racecourse. Suffice to say, everything fell into place with the resurrection of these bed races around the VAMC parade grounds. Not that I am bragging, but my team triumphed in this bedlam.

Following an eventful year on the job, my position got converted to permanent status and included the added titles of patient representative and EEO advisor. Soon afterward, a promotion was granted, and duties expanded to include special outreach programming for Native American veterans, homeless veterans, and women veterans. My position also resulted in appointments to the boards of three community service organizations. I even joined the employee bowling league, but had to give up on staff volleyball due to deficient depth perception that too often translated into volleys bouncing off my forehead.

One of my most cherished projects involved organizing a cavalry reenactment for the state of Washington centennial, which brought back to these hallowed grounds, troops of skirmishing blue-coated soldiers, marching formations, gun salutes, flag ceremonies, saber drills, white canvas tents, campfires, horse patrols, an authentic Gatling gun, and the daily bugling of reveille.

My regular duties included coordinating community events at this campus. The one square mile of property occupied by this VAMC was expansive enough to kick off hot air balloon launches for the annual Walla Walla Balloon Stampede and host the yearly Reid Brothers Circus. Influenced by my escapades of running, I also added to these historic grounds a local 5K fun run called the Cavalry Charge.

Just as enriching in this job were the outreach ventures into the Native American homelands of the Nez Perce, Umatilla, and Yakima nations. Added to this list of tough assignments was the annual escorting of VA patients to the world-famous Pendleton Roundup. Because this rodeo endeavor required the donning of a cowboy hat and boots, I thus evolved into a Yosemite Sam of sorts. "*Consarnit*" and "*Dagnabbit*," you just do what you've got to do, out here on the range.

During the ensuing years, my public relations efforts paid off well enough to earn two national awards and several regional commendations. This also caught the attention of other VA medical centers, one of which was the Reno facility in Northwest Nevada. Following continuous coercion by an assertive service chief named, Jerry, I accepted a promotion and gambled on another Wild-West rendezvous. While now moving on and moving up, perhaps the past stereotypes, struggles, and Magoo moments had finally been overcome.

Gone like the Wind

Putting the pedal to the mettle is what drives life.

Within each of us is that drive to drive. For some, however, climbing behind the wheel and putting the pedal to the metal might challenge common sense. However, you sometimes just have to throw caution to the wind and sandblast your way through life. At least, that's the way my brother Tom, and I saw it, right before reaching new heights and then crash-landing.

While still residing in the Great Northwest, I invited Tom to fly out from Wisconsin and join me for some Pacific coast adventuring. Neither of us knew what lie ahead and was to come. With our wives joining us, we piled into a Subaru wagon and headed for the Oregon coast. Our expectations were nothing more than beachcombing and possible glimpses of sea lions. A nefarious jaunt over hill and dale was never anticipated. Nonetheless, we luckily survived to tell this story.

Once reaching the coast, a whole new world showcased itself in the endless beaches, sculptured rock formations, and rollicking waves. It was the immense sand dunes, however, which, like Sirens, seduced us into doing something unimaginable and way beyond outlandish. Just like me, Tom inherited the same faulty headlights and insurmountable barrier to a driver's license. This prohibition, of course, does not necessarily prevent one from driving. There are alternatives, one of which routinely appeared on the touristy billboards dotting this panoramic coastline.

Unbeknownst to us, we were about to enter a land both enchanted and ominous. Lying in wait were hazardous quicksand, waterlogged deflation plains, tree islands, and knoblike mounds called hummocks. The dunes themselves carried monikers such as grass-capped foredunes, transverse slipface sands, parabola blowouts, and monster obliques towering up to 180 feet. This midsection of the state's coastline comprised the Oregon Dunes National Recreation Area. It represented a barren geological stretch occupied by only two tenants, scrub pines and sand rebels. According to the roadside signs, everyone was invited to become one of the later.

Although apprehensive, our entourage finally relinquished to the unrelenting coercion and pulled into one of the dune buggy rentals. As we exited the car to explore this idea, the burly proprietor, who I dubbed "Dunemaster," stepped away from a monster sand machine he was working on. His shoulder-length blonde hair, bandanna headband, tie-dyed tank top, and tattered jeans made him a throwback from the 1960's. Walking awkwardly with a noticeable limp, the Dunemaster toured us around his enterprise while crusading on the virtues of dune buggies. He noted that this shop got started after his return from a U.S. Army tour in Vietnam. This military veteran then emphasized how dune buggies helped to suppress the anger and stress of his wartime experiences.

It did not take the Dunemaster long to convince us that this was something we just had to do. Besides, he made no

mention that a driver's license or driving experience was required. Within minutes, the waivers were signed, and three naïve souls were strapped securely into what the proprietor called Odysseys. These desert vehicles are basically one man dune buggies powered by a 250cc engine. Wrapped around and above you, a sturdy roll bar serves as an additional safeguard. Not only are the helmeted drivers secured with seat belts and shoulder straps, but even their hands also become fastened to the steering wheel. This was to prevent you from sticking your arm out and bracing during any misfortunate rollover. All of this seemed to make sense to us, except for Tom's skeptical wife, who opted not to participate in this foolhardy endeavor.

Like the adventurous Three Musketeers, Tom, Dianna, and I proceeded onward and upward into the sandy mountains. With no speed limits, no traffic signs, and no maps to follow, this was pretty much the perfect setting for out of sight drivers. Without hesitation, we then blasted off, or at least I should say, that is what Tom did. When approaching the very first dune, he floored it and rocketed to the top. When I tried the same fearless maneuver at a much slower speed, I began sliding sideways and decided quickly to traverse around the hill rather than risk a back-flipping rollover. Perhaps this might have been a good lesson for Tom, who was, by far, too much of a motorized daredevil.

Once out in the cascading dunes, it did not take long for everyone to separate into different directions. Being early in the tourist season, we had this wonderland all to ourselves. Darting in and out of these dunes, we occasionally passed each other and sometimes attempted a game of "catch me if you can." The rental covered one hour of motoring about, and our intentions were to make use of every minute. However, it did not take long to begin feeling the repeated jarring impacts from bouncing over the drifts and sometimes going airborne.

Deciding to take a break from all the jolts, I stopped my

buggy to listen and look around me. Surprisingly, the only sound audible was that of Dianna's approaching buggy. As for Tom, no sight or sound of him existed. After discussing this conundrum with Dianna, we began an anxious search. Advancing over the crest of a sizable dune, we suddenly came upon a forlorn figure plodding through the grainy sands. It was Tom marching like a nomadic Bedouin, whose camel had broken down and left him stranded. I pulled up to him and asked the obvious question as to the whereabouts of his dune buggy. After some momentary dawdling, Tom finally fessed up and answered, "It's in a tree!" When I retorted back about his hitting a tree, Tom calmly corrected me by replying, "I didn't hit a tree. I landed in one!"

Being perplexed, I crawled out of my buggy and followed Tom to the top of an awesome dune. On the other side of this summit was a wooded area of scrub pines known as a tree island. These were gnarly stunted conifers, which somehow found a way to survive in the sands. Small splotches of these needled trees were scattered throughout the dunes. However, this piney patch was different than all others. It featured a dune buggy, mounted prominently and firmly upon its crown.

From my brief experience in this sport, I fully understood Tom as he explained how his buggy had become perched. To ascend the biggest of dunes, you have to charge full throttle to the top and anticipate the buggy sliding down the other side. Unable to brake in the shifting sand, Tom's momentum launched him onto the top of a scrub pine. Now lodged within the tree's twisted and tough branches, this begrudging pine was not about to let go.

Although Dianna, Tom, and I collectively tried to free the buggy, it would not budge. In the midst of this dilemma, the Three Musketeers had now been reduced to the Three Stooges. When it became apparent that additional help was needed, I departed from this fiasco and headed back to seek out the Dunemaster. Along the way, I began thinking about how the

Dunemaster might react and what impact this situation would have on his war-related stress. I also wondered about those waiver and liability forms we had signed without carefully reviewing.

Paranoid about the inevitable, I slowly pulled into the Dunemaster's repair shop, drew a deep breath, and nervously noted that a buggy had gotten sort of stuck. The Dunemaster then stroked his chin stubble and muttered something while proceeding to load tow chains into what resembled a jet-engine dragster. As he revved up his fuel-injected buggy, it sounded altogether as menacing as it looked. Tailgating my lead, his supercharged sand machine rumbled behind me. Fearing the worst, I imagined being steamrolled by his monstrosity and pummeled into the sands. Perhaps he was only waiting for me to guide him to the entangled buggy, where, years later, three unidentified bodies would be discovered buried in chains and mummified within the dunes.

A sense of doom engulfed me as we arrived at the base of the cursed site. With considerable effort and a whole lot of grumbling, the Dunemaster limped through the loose steep sands. Reaching the crest with chains in hand, he stared intensely at the pine with the impaled buggy. As the Dunemaster scrutinized this hapless scene, a long drawn-out moment of silence followed. His entranced stare and scowl further emphasized his mood. In what seemed like a vindictive pause, he now appeared to be contemplating our impending demise. What happened next, however, will never be forgotten.

After breaking his silence with an exaggerated exhale, the Dunemaster turned to Tom and said, "Damn, that's where they usually put them." He then slid down to the treetop debacle, attached the chains, and ambled back to his behemoth buggy. Revving up this sand dragster once again and edging forward, Tom's entrapped Odyssey soon came free from its perch. As Tom inspected the buggy, brushed away some pine needles, and detached the chains, the Dunemaster walked over to him. What all of us now expected was the impending onslaught of obscenities and a stern lecture. Instead, the tie-dyed war vet just looked at us and said, "Being that you were parked so long in that tree, go ahead and add some extra time to your ride." With that, we spent the rest of our excursion conservatively tooling about. Gone like the wind, our debuts as high flying kites had now come down to earth.

From what has been described, most would consider it crazy that Tom and I dared to engage in this seaside malarkey. Because of an entirely different perspective, we really do not see it that way. As previously noted, within each of us is that drive to drive. Granted, this sometimes creates waves, which just happens to remind me. I recently heard about jet-ski rentals at a nearby lake. No roads to confine you, no stop signs to watch for, and, better yet, no perilous trees to contend with. "Heavens to Murgatroyd" and "Jumping Jehosaphat," this most definitely sounds like another enticing adventure.

The Knight before Christmas

Providing good cheer and friendship makes each of us a magical elf.

Yes, Virginia, there really is a Santa Claus. This I know for certain, because of personally meeting the jolly ol' elf. He is every bit both magical and merry. Just for the record, however, his real name is Bill; and when on leave from the North Pole, he actually resides in Nevada.

Changing workplaces usually comes with new expectations, new adventures, and new friends. I experienced a landslide of all three upon transferring to Reno. Some of this, I anticipated. However, working alongside Santa, was not one of them. Yet, despite this now being summertime in the high desert of the Sierra foothills, there he stood in my office doorway on the fourth day into this new government job. Although absent of the scarlet wool suit and hat, there was no mistaking this rotund figure with the flowing white beard, wire-rimmed spectacles, and bright red suspenders. He was the real deal, and because my office lacked a fireplace and chimney, this walk-in approach of his was the most practical option.

Thinking inquisitively about déjà vu, a not-so-distant memory began resurfacing. Hadn't I been through something like this before? No one is going to fool me again with another newcomer game of hide and seek. If this guy wants to proclaim a "ho, ho, ho" and merrily announce that he is here with a sleigh load of reindeer hides, well, so be it.

Little did I know that having Santa Claus appear before me represented only the tip of the iceberg, My stint at this new place and time would eventually entail a cast of characters representing war heroes, crusty old cowboys, corporate moguls, street people, a former vaudeville performer, a mobster, a Hollywood extra, a Shakey's pizza baron, a triple-tread submarine vet named "Bay Leaves," and even the first jet pilot to break the sound barrier. Added to this menagerie was bakery man Harry, who every so often, mysteriously dropped by my office to leave a loaf of bread and then quickly vanish. There were also two genuine angels named Margaret and Miriam. Other cast members included one-armed Eddie, preacher Vince, Scammy, Gunny, Chicago Joe, Olympic torch-runner Dick, Ruth and Ruth, muleskinner Gene, timeless Annabel, Kitten, Robert the comic (who once performed with Abbot and Costello), lovable Virgil, a Scrooge impersonator, the Lake Almanor tree haulers, and, of course, my trusted confidants and close friends, Doberman Dave and Major Ralph. Therefore, among this collage, a midsummer Santa was just the beginning of things to come.

Because this Santa preferred to be called Bill, I had no problem honoring his request. No one is in a position to argue with the one and only, plump purveyor of Christmas. I had to wonder, however, why the heck is this venerable holiday celebrity here to see me? As such, I asked and got a response not anticipated. Good ol' Santa, or Bill I should say, already knew that my headlights were not up to par and needed technical assistance. He assured me that I was about to get wired. Bill had a considerable expertise in adaptive computer technology and now wanted to introduce me to every bit of it, no pun intended. So there you have it. Not only had I become acquainted with the great gnome of the North Pole, I got to learn he was a full-fledged geek as well. Perhaps I would soon find out that Rudolph's red nose resulted from an imbedded computer chip and how the annual Christmas Eve trek was just a matter of fully integrated GPS. It would not have surprised me to discover a sleigh equipped with a DVD player and hands-free technology.

It did not take long to realize Bill's incredible role. He had been coming to the medical center for years and assisting vets as a volunteer. This guy personified both a complete computer nut and wily wizard. He set up a computer lab right in the hospital to teach disabled veterans who were undergoing recovery and needed a respite from four-wall confinement. For patients unable to leave their rooms, Bill also created a portable computer unit that could be transported to the bedside. The mobile system was used to not only teach these veterans computer skills, but also to allow them to send e-mails, design greeting cards, and explore the Internet from their bedsides.

At the time I first met Bill, computer science was still in its infancy. Bill spent both night and day tinkering with new devices and programs that most of us had never heard of. There were times when the medical center's information technology staff got perturbed over Bill's ability to troubleshoot complicated glitches, which they could not resolve. These feds just don't like you meddling with their electronic toys. Bill's greatest passion, however, was reaching out to persons with varying challenges and introducing them to specialized assistive equipment. No matter where or when needed, Bill never hesitated to help. But then again, this was Santa.

As a magical elf, Bill had a mischievous side to him as well. Knowing that my secretary, Mary, did not share his same passion for technology, he often programmed a cartoon greeting onto her office computer. Upon arriving and turning on her system, a laughing and dancing character appeared on the monitor. Neither amused nor quite sure on how to rid herself of this animation, Mary would begin grumbling as to who let Bill into our office.

To further certify his Santa status, Bill always showed up in the "Saint Nick of Time." As I began building a military heritage museum within this VA medical center, Bill somehow acquired the hard-to-find mannequins that I desperately needed. It made for quite a sight to see this bearded wonder carrying naked plastic bodies down the hospital corridors.

Due to extreme modesty, Bill actually covered over parts of the female mannequin with computer paper.

Anytime Bill found out about an upcoming ceremony or other special events, his desktop publishing skills kicked in to design posters and bulletins. He also dabbled in something called digital photography, before most of us even heard about this newfangled horizon. As a senior whiz kid, Bill even owned one of the first satellite phones, which did not resemble anything like those of today. This retired civil engineer, who battled type 1 diabetes, suffered a previous heart attack, and twice lost his home to fires, only worried about what he could do for others. This also translated into adopting a burro named Babe, who lived in Bill's backyard. Perhaps Babe was the emergency backup for Rudolph. Throughout many years, Bill and his wife, Evelyn, cared for dozens of foster children, which I strongly suspect were actually elves-in-training.

Whenever the winter holiday season rolled around, Bill turned to a more traditional role. Both he and Evelyn donned all the customary Mr. and Mrs. Claus attire. From Thanksgiving to Christmas, the two of them showed up at shopping malls, churches, schools, healthcare centers, and, of course in this gaming town, casinos. To top all this off, every patient in the Reno VA medical center got a personal Christmas Eve visit from Santa as well. Together, Bill and I started an annual project called the Angel Tree. It involved two dozen needy children from a nearby elementary school. These students were escorted to a medical center party and then presented a mountain of Christmas gifts by the staff. While Bill handed out hugs and presents, I strummed my guitar and led the children in holiday songs.

As chance would have it, Bill did not represent the only Christmas character at this VA medical center. Adding to the wintertime fanfare was a guy named Richard, who worked in the hospital's laundry room. Whenever the blustery snows began to fall, Richard mysteriously showed up at holiday venues. Attired in a Victorian stovepipe top hat, long woolen overcoat, and dapper neck scarf, Richard was the spitting-image of Ebenezer Scrooge. Both Richard's ruffled crown of hair and the rim of his chin were frosted white. His wire-rimmed spectacles, ruddy complexion, and slightly pointed nose, brought the stingy elder of Dickens fame to life. Undaunted by any ghost of Marley, his true personality was quite the opposite of a genuine Scrooge. Rather than a formidable scowl, this imposter all too often betrayed a miserly persona with mischievous grins and a charitable soul. Richard continually organized employee events such as Mash Days, ugly necktie/hat contests, bowling tournaments, and community fundraisers. In every respect, Richard had the same heart of gold as Bill.

Although Santa season continued year-round for Bill, he equally reveled in being an everyday bona fide geek. Bill's passion for CRT's, CPU's, zip drives, and other IT gizmos got fueled by his background in mechanical and electrical engineering. While many of his peers became discombobulated by the rapidly evolving technology, this became Bill's calling. Not only was Bill infatuated with learning everything he could about this science, but he also needed to share each of his incredible discoveries.

Bill's high-tech tutoring introduced me to a mind-boggling world of enhanced text software, screen readers, and flatbed scanners. At first, I shied away from all the intimidation that computers represented. Bill, however, never slowed down in his ongoing pursuit to apply a technology solution to every challenge. Although he did not manage to convert me to geek status, my ability to level the playing field and electronically succeed was due to his patience, persistence, and touch of magic.

More than just a tutor, Bill became one of my best friends. When my daughter, Brianna, was adopted, she gained an additional set of grandparents, Bill and Evelyn. Like so many others, Brianna always wanted to tug on Bill's beard and test its authenticity. During Brianna's first three years, every Christmas Eve merited personal visits from a red velvet suited Santa Claus, who came bearing gifts galore. To our family, this forever-smiling character became Sir Bill, the knight before Christmas.

In a circumstance that is somewhat difficult to explain, I opted in 1998 for early retirement from the VA system. Federal government downsizing, buyout incentives, and my disability status, all contributed to the decision. This turn of events, then led to an exchange of the Sierras for the Cascades. It was time to leave Reno and head to a place called Bend, Oregon. Breaking the news to Bill and Evelyn would be incredibly difficult. After so many years of such close friendship, how do you say good-bye to Mr. and Mrs. Claus?

When our house sold much quicker than anticipated, my family and I suddenly found ourselves uprooting in the midst of the December holiday season. On the night before our

exodus, Bill surprised us by stopping by our home in full Santa regalia and carrying a huge sack full of presents. During this visit, however, I noticed an unusual bulge in his red velvet coat pocket. When the bulge started wiggling, I instantly suspected what he was sneakily up to. Bill then reached into his pocket and out popped a black miniature poodle puppy named Barney. This gift-giver was never short on surprises, especially the one that came almost exactly a year later.

After my move to central Oregon, Bill and I kept routinely in touch. I could not look at my computer without missing this character. If that wasn't enough of a reminder, Brianna's packed room of toys showed off Bill's generosity with an entire collection of porcelain dolls, numerous trolls with neon hair, and, of course, Bill's favorite fuzzy critters that sing obnoxiously whenever squeezed. Just weeks before Christmas 1999 in our new setting, a huge box arrived. Seeing that it had come from Nevada, I knew that Bill was back in seasonal form. This time he really went overboard. We had known Bill's gifting to include three to four presents each Christmas for Brianna. Upon opening this box, however, it became immediately obvious that Bill had gone all out. After removing the colorfully wrapped gifts, the count added up to seventeen. This was unbelievable, and I began wondering as to why Bill sent so many presents this time.

The next day, just when I prepared to dial Bill's number and thank him, my telephone rang. At the other end of the line quivered the voice of his wife, Evelyn. Right away, I knew something was terribly wrong. She then told me that Bill had suffered a severe heart attack the day before and never recovered. Less than an hour ago, Bill had passed away. This became one of the saddest days in my life. Santa was now gone, something I could not even imagine.

After this saddening phone call, I turned to look at the enormous number of gifts sent to us by Bill. This precious stack of presents barely fit beneath our Christmas tree. Staring at them, I could not help but think that he somehow knew this would be his very last Christmas. As such, Bill unloaded the entire sleigh for his Christmas finale.

Over the years, Mrs. Claus has carried on Bill's legacy of generosity and compassion. Not a holiday goes by without Brianna receiving cards or presents from Evelyn. Through her ongoing generosity, the spirit and memory of Bill lives on.

A character like Bill is never forgotten or replaced. Each year when strolling through the shopping malls at Christmas time, I pause when seeing a familiar white-bearded and red-suited gentleman, anchoring the bright colored holiday throne. Prominently seated before a lineup of wide-eyed children, his belly laughs begin to awaken so many recollections of mine. A temptation always beckons to push through the crowd and ask him about some current computer glitches that are troubling me. I hesitate momentarily, because there is only one Bill and this impersonator represents nothing more than a Santa look-alike.

Fortunately, I got to know Bill well, but far from long enough. This jolly gentleman is dearly missed each and every day. Because of him, I learned wisely that the real value of Christmas and life cannot truly be assessed until you get a Bill from Santa.

The Taming of the Shrewd

A simple fix often comes from where you least expect it.

Meeting Michael began with a pledge of secrecy and a serious attitude change. Perhaps the word *confidentiality* would be more appropriate than *secrecy*. Regardless of what you call it, my shrewdness needed refurbishing and the repeal of a whole lot of prejudice. And because of a character named John, I would now see Michael from an enlightened point of view.

Remaining from those past years as a country hick, the redness of my neck had not yet worn off. So when several college buddies tried to tell me that my new friend John was gay, I suspected trickery. Just because I came from a small town without any real acquaintance to gay persons, no assumption should be made about me being too naïve to identify someone of this orientation. As a greenhorn freshman, I was nowhere near that dumb. Living four doors down the hall from me, John seemed like just another dorm resident. Although this Milwaukee kid did have a funny look about him, he couldn't be that kind of "funny guy."

At six foot five and weighing no more than 150 pounds, John was a lanky figure stretched out of proportion. Nothing he wore seemed to fit him right. This skinny dude had absolutely no meat on his bones. As such, this beanstalk with the dirty-blonde hair and scruffy beard became dubbed "Iguana" at my White Hall dormitory. Not only were John and I part of the same dorm, but we also attended the same zoology class and lab.

John was both different and interesting. Unlike me, he had no connection to sports. Instead, John touted a passion for music and the arts, which consistently clashed with his science studies. His family sent him to college to follow in his father's footsteps as a dentist. The plan was to start at UW-Whitewater and then transfer to Marquette University. Although John had begun college by conceding to these family wishes, dentistry would never be a part of his future. Deeply troubled by this career pressure, John also faced an even greater struggle to cope with his own identity.

One step into John's dorm room set him apart. The walls were covered with colored foil, black-light posters, and curious illustrations. Incense and candles burned constantly. Statues and other art pieces crowded the bookshelves. A funky wind chime hung in front of his window. More often than not, a Moody Blues album was cranked up on the stereo. His eclectic surroundings looked as if he had raided a Spencer's gifts store.

From what I learned during my redneck upbringing, gay guys were petite and effeminate types. They talk in a weird way as well. John, however, represented a big gangly dude with a Lincoln-like face and ordinary voice. Besides all this, John had a girlfriend. In fact, he had several, although none of them became serous companions. Nonetheless, there were women in his life. Even a hayseed like me knew that gay guys don't have girlfriends.

John and I hitchhiked a couple of times to Madison and Milwaukee. The Madison trip was to hang out with his older sister, who attempted teaching me bump dancing to disco music. The Milwaukee trek led to his family home, where I got to meet the most domineering of mothers and John's attractive younger sibling, Gina. When John sensed that his sister had caught my eye, he made every effort to discourage me from having anything to do with her. This, however, was not the first time John so actively tried to separate me from the opposite sex. My future wife participated in the same zoology class and lab that John and I attended. Once Dianna and I started dating, John became intent on keeping me from any serious relationship with her. Knowing what I now know, John was intensely jealous.

During my sophomore year, I remained in the dorm, while John moved off campus. I stopped by his apartment periodically to visit him. Keeping a storehouse of food always on hand, John's pad served as a magnet to starving students like me. I still remember the time when I pigged out by consuming almost an entire toasted loaf of bread smothered with raspberry jam. John just sat there laughing while poking fun at my hog-wild ways. As a city slicker, this is what John expected from a country bumpkin such as me.

My visits to John's became fewer and further apart as I began to notice the changes in this guy. John had turned to drugs like the seedy characters now frequenting his apartment. When it finally sank in that some of the hardcore dopers hanging out with John might actually be boyfriends, I wanted nothing more to do with him. No matter how humorous, intellectual, and interesting he was, I scorned any association with this peculiar situation. My friends were right about John. He had finally come completely out of the closet. As for me, I felt embarrassed and betrayed. During my final years of college, I rarely caught sight of John again.

Several months after graduation, I attended the wedding of my junior year roommate, Kurt. As friends sat around talking about our college days, somehow John's name came up. When I asked whatever became of this guy, another former roommate paused and looked at me. He then sheepishly stated, "John hung himself two months ago." I was shocked. As another square peg finding it hard to fit in, John's experiences were not so different from mine, and yet, ironically, I projected toward him the same prejudices that often plagued me. No one is immune, and most of us are guilty of bias.

Over the years, I've thought about what really happened to John. He did not commit suicide, but instead was murdered by bigotry. Like my redneck buddies, I often used the word *faggot* and other derogatory terms when referring to gay persons. None of us made life easy for John. He did not fit into our world. For this reason, he turned to drugs and other dark paths as an escape. When that did not work, he chose a more fatal solution. Yet, for what it is worth, the novelty of John helped to open my narrow mind. As such, I was not about to let a new friend named Michael endure any of the similar bonehead prejudice.

Upon beginning my public affairs position at the Reno VA Medical Center, I got acquainted with an intriguing cast of characters. My boss Jerry and I coordinated a crew of over 350 volunteers. Jerry believed in creating opportunities for anyone and everyone to serve the military veterans at this facility. Coming from all walks of life, these volunteers ranged from bank vice presidents to homeless persons. Regardless of how different their backgrounds represented, every one of them shared a passion to lend a helping hand. Michael was no exception.

Describing Michael is somewhat difficult. Average in height, weight, and build, he further accented his ordinary look with the daily attire of a T-shirt and shorts. On formal occasions, however, Michael would resort to a polo shirt and slightly faded blue jeans. At thirty-something, his clean-shaven baby face of bright eyes and a perennial smile, often fooled others into thinking he was much younger. This guy's always cheerful disposition never betrayed any personal hardships.

After first being introduced to Michael, I soon learned of his phenomenal abilities to fix almost anything. A short time later, Jerry pulled me aside to talk about this particular volunteer. Speaking in strict confidence, Jerry wanted me to know that Michael was HIV positive. Although this was a private matter that did not need to be openly shared with staff and volunteers, Jerry felt I should be informed, just in case the rumor mill went haywire or any symptoms began surfacing with Michael.

At first, I was not sure how to deal with the circumstance. Never before had I met anyone with this stigmatized disease. My ignorance and prejudices needed immediate recalibrating. Personal concerns about the safety of our patients, staff, and Michael as well, were eventually quelled through some research and consultation. However, I still needed an understanding as to how Michael's predicament came to be. According to the good ol' boys network, HIV was a payback plague within the gay community. By now, I had overcome my own redneck past to understand otherwise. In this particular situation, Michael had, years before, made the mistake of partying a bit too much. While overindulged on alcohol, he shared a needle that was being passed around. Five years later, the diagnosis of HIV came to light. Although full-blown AIDS had not yet surfaced, it was on the horizon. So there you have it. Even folks, who are not gay, can and do get AIDS.

When Michael began as a volunteer, he showed few signs of any illness. His personality and willingness to help everyone made him one of the most popular volunteers. Many of us took advantage of the fact that Michael was a master handyman. Being a mechanical miracle worker, he could fix anything from cars to washing machines and sprinkler systems. Because of this talent, Jerry and I often enlisted Michael as a combined house-sitter and dog-sitter, when either of us went on extended vacations. We did so knowing that while away, Michael would repair whatever needed attention. We also took this step to give Michael more comfortable surroundings than he was accustomed to. There were times when Michael lived either in his station wagon or at a tiny converted garage. As far as I knew, Michael did not have a regular job and seemed to be living on minimal public assistance. However, this never appeared to bother Michael. He still remains the most trustworthy and non materialistic person I've ever met.

Just a few years after getting to know Michael, two events changed the world around me. My boss Jerry got a promotion and moved to Los Angeles. At the same time, Michael's HIV spiraled into AIDS. While Jerry had been such a close friend to Michael, I doubted myself as being equally capable. However, I was not going to let Michael down. Together with my office secretary Mary, the two of us watched over our mutual friend. As Michael's predicament worsened, his ability to continue as a volunteer diminished. Instead of caring for others, it was Michael who now needed serious caretaking. When word spread that he had AIDS, the adversity of this dilemma became even more formidable. The questions and comments about Michael's illness and character turned into an ugly ordeal. After being admitted to a local nursing home, many friends now shied away from Michael. Even the staff of this long term care center had reservations about visitations. Oftentimes I was asked if I actually wanted to enter his room and see him. Upon doing so, confusion then erupted over whether I needed to glove-up, gown-over, and be masked.

Although Michael required daily nursing care, he seemed marooned as a young man in this elderly oriented place. It bothered me immensely to see someone of my same age in such a gloomy predicament and knowing that it would only worsen over time. Upon visits, I oftentimes found him sitting isolated in a wheelchair and parked in the far corner of the activity room. Something definitely had to be done about this estrangement.

With the annual Reno/Sparks Ribfest coming up on Labor Day, I got medical permission for Michael to join me for an outing and a brew. At this stage, the two of us absolutely needed a drink. On the first day of the festival, Dianna and I showed up at Michael's nursing home. Michael was both anxious and excited to depart from this setting. With considerable effort, Michael managed to pull himself into our van's middle section. I then lifted his wheelchair and placed it in the back. Following our arrival to this summer-ending event, we took in the free Nitty Gritty Dirt Band concert outside the Nugget Casino.

While doing so, Michael and I consumed both the music and a beer or two. A short while later, Michael needed a pit stop. As I waited outside the casino's restroom, a crashing sound was suddenly heard. Michael had tumbled out of his wheelchair. Rushing in and attempting to help him, I came to grips with just how frail he had become from this disease. Upon getting Michael back to the van, Dianna and I had to lift him into the back storage area. Even with our assistance, he simply did not have the strength to step up into one of the van seats.

Although I did not know it at the time, this would be Michael's last excursion beyond the care center. In the weeks that followed, I tried to frequently visit Michael. Something miraculously happened, however, which interrupted this routine. After five years of hopes and disappointments in the adoption process, Dianna and I suddenly became the proud parents of a one week-old baby girl, whom we named Brianna. The last we had heard from the adoption agency, left us believing that our long wait would continue indefinitely. Instead, we got a twenty-four-hour notice on parenthood. Life now became a mixture of blessings and childcare chaos.

When I broke the good news to Michael, he turned giddy and almost rolled out of bed. Unbeknownst to us, Michael then shared that he too was adopted and had an adopted sister, Amy, as well. Both were raised by an affluent family, who lived adjacent to a world-famous golf course. Never before had Michael mentioned his family and background. He had always been extremely private about his past. Our little girl's arrival brought to light, another side of Michael. The balance between his fading and Brianna's blossoming now seemed to put Michael at peace.

From this point forward, every visit to Michael involved conversations about Brianna. He wanted to know all about her and how she was doing each day. In many ways, he acted like the beaming uncle of his first and most favorite niece. During this period, I got to meet Michael's family from California.

Together, all of us sadly watched as Michael's health continued to deteriorate. The day finally came when I received a call to rush immediately to the nursing home. Michael's breathing now faltered as he drifted in and out of consciousness. As I entered his room, my depleted friend lay motionless in his bed. I touched his arm and let Michael know I was there beside him. There was no reaction. I waited alongside him, not knowing what to do or say. I really do not recall how much time I spent in his room on this day. When eventually noting to Michael that I now had to leave, he surprised me by opening his eyes. In a faint voice that was barely audible, he softly spoke out, "Take good care of that little girl Brianna." With my eyes tearing up and speech quivering, I then answered back, "'I'll do just that, Michael."

After leaving Michael's room, I quickly rushed back home to deal with my thoughts and spend some extensive time with Brianna. I no sooner walked through the door when my phone rang. It was one of Michael's family members sharing the inevitable somber news. Michael had passed away just moments after I left his room. God needed a master handyman, and now Michael was on his way.

Without a doubt, Michael was one cool guy, whose life ended far too soon. What I will always remember about remarkable Michael is that he could repair nearly everything, and yet, what he fixed most of all for me was my attitude about others. Because of Michael, and John as well, I no longer judge people so quickly. Both lent themselves to the taming of the shrewd. Due to these two characters, my prejudices have been adjusted and some altogether eliminated. What I feel specifically in regard to Michael, however, is that Brianna, now and forever, has a guardian angel who can fix just about anything.

One Flew out of the Cuckoo's Nest

Although it may be said that birds of a feather flock together, a strange bird landing in the nest, will surely ruffle feathers until someone flies the coop.

Don't ever let down your guard. Just when everything seems to be going well and you are at the top of your game, watch out. The players may suddenly change and so, too, the rules. You then discover that what really counts is not what work you do or where it is done, but rather who you work for and with.

As my boss at the Reno VA Medical Center, Jerry was an incredible mentor. We shared so many similar ideas, yet often differed in our approaches. I learned so much from him, and quite possibly, he garnered a few lessons from me as well. He was one of the best bosses I had ever worked for and ran this department like a ministry. Overseeing the volunteer and public affairs programs at this VAMC, Jerry practiced an open door and welcome-in policy for anyone willing to contribute. Sometimes this got him into trouble by reaching out and including volunteers that others did not wish to accommodate. And when some of these not so conventional volunteers needed assistance as well, Jerry never hesitated to lend them a helping hand. This oftentimes translated into loaning out his truck, providing an extra meal, or just spending time listening to their life stories.

Over the years, Jerry built up a volunteer workforce that numbered in the hundreds and accounted for over sixty thousand hours of services annually. This entourage ranged from curious young students to wise old elders. Assisting alongside the medical center staff were retired professionals, college interns, middle and high school students, homemakers, civic club members, and military veterans. No one from any walk of life was exempt. As such, Jerry's brigade also included street people, recovering addicts and alcoholics, physically and mentally challenged individuals, court-referred community service workers, unlucky high-rollers, and a fair share of lonely hearts.

A personal mission of Jerry's was to involve youth at this VAMC. Although the youth volunteer activities he started, resulted in numerous awards from Sertoma and other civic groups, there were grumblings at times, about this place becoming a baby-sitting center for juvenile delinquents. One particular episode almost changed the image of this gaming town VAMC. Known as the Escort office, this program provided daily volunteers who escorted patients and supplies throughout the medical center. All any staff had to do, was call into this office, and a volunteer would be dispatched immediately to assist them.

Wanting to get the youth more involved, it was decided that perhaps one of these young volunteers would be capable of manning the Escort office phone. It just so happened that the teenage girl chosen to take on this role, insisted on identifying herself by her nickname. Therefore, when staff began calling the Escort office on this teen's first day, the soft and sultry voice on the other end of the line answered, "Escort office, this is Kitten"!

Being an innovator, Jerry introduced the arts world to this medical center. He somehow arranged for a patient to paint military murals on the interior walls of the veterans' nursing home. As a result, there were historic warplanes flying about and battleships cruising down the corridors. Hauling it across town in his pickup, Jerry also managed to place an eclectic iron sculpture on the VAMC grounds, which then served as a Vietnam War memorial. Doing all this, however, often met with some staunch bureaucratic resistance. Nonetheless, Jerry persisted.

Jerry's ingenuity also showed up in other ways. On the top floor of this hospital, he set up a ham radio system, for hospitalized veterans with operators' licenses, to use during their inpatient stays. In one of the center's main corridors, Jerry created a Hall of Fame to recognize all the VA's supporting casts. He also initiated the groundwork to develop the Veterans Hospital Foundation. This organization then purchased a property across from the VAMC and turned it into what became the Spouse House, a no charge residence serving the families and friends of patients.

By his example of inclusion, Jerry opened up an entire new world to me. Coincidentally, his success opened a new world to him as well. Four years after my working alongside Jerry, he accepted the challenge of testing his skills with a promotion to the VAMC in Los Angeles. With this California center being one of the flagship facilities in the system, the opportunity became too hard to resist. After seventeen years in Reno, Jerry was headed for the other side of the Sierras.

Jerry's departure was hard on me and about to become even more difficult than anticipated. Upon his transfer, he recommended me for his now vacant position. Although my current and former positions were marked by accolades, I was about to learn a bureaucratic lesson about the oftentimes irrational nature of the federal government. Suffice to say, Jerry's former job got wrangled by a Texas gal with lesser experience, minimal education, and few successes. Clued in by one of the selection committee members, discrepancies started surfacing. Miffed by the runaround and given no explanation for this bamboozling, I began questioning the process. When I got wind of what appeared to be some skullduggery, I exercised my right to file a formal complaint through the EEOC. Almost immediately, the "you-know-what," hit the fan. The medical center director took this action personally, and the backlash ensued. Being naïve to this circumstance, I did not know that a huge can of worms had now opened, nor did I realize that the process of investigating my complaint would drag on for almost three years. All this transpired, due to a lack of straight answers.

When Jerry's replacement came on board as my new boss, this lady immediately lambasted me at length for contesting the appointment process. In what appeared to be additional retaliation, she then ordered me to vacate my current workspace and move into a small hallway office. After noting to her that I needed to make arrangements for removing and reconnecting my adaptive computer system, she went into a tirade that questioned any need for this specialized equipment. Although futile, I tried to explain my unique situation and the resulting required accommodations. This supervisor would have none of it and acted as if I was trying to pull one over on her. With Santa Bill just happening to be in the area at this time, I asked him to sit in on this debate. With that, she sternly chastised Bill by telling him that he had no business assisting me with computers or anything else. At this point, not only had she demeaned me, but also insulted Bill as well. He later referred to her as a mad bull in a china shop. To me, this new supervisor seemed like the cantankerous queen from *Alice in Wonderland*, always angry and ready to behead anyone around her.

Unfortunately, the antagonistic situation was not about to get any better. Many of the volunteers such as Bill had become close friends of mine, which then led to them being blacklisted by this newly appointed manager. It was almost as if she had come into this position, branding me as her enemy and paranoid of anyone on my side. Most of all, she acted suspicious as to the legitimacy of my faulty headlights.

Several times this supervisor would enter my office, hold up a memo, and then inquire as to what the document was all about. Upon my response that I could not identify the writing from a distance, she taunted back, "Oh, that's right. You don't see very well." She attempted a similar tactic at staff meetings by asking me to identify people on the far side of the room.

My inability to do so resulted in her same commentary. I sensed things were really getting bad when one day she grilled me about my speaking engagements for the medical center. When I explained to her that outreach venues were a major component of my public affairs duties, she shocked me by proclaiming that anyone unable to drive should not be a public speaker. Of course, this was the same lady who later told me that the reason for limited numbers of African Americans in the navy is because they generally are incapable of swimming. Her off-the-wall remarks became commonplace. She appeared to have all kinds of biased hang-ups relating to a myriad of subjects. Unfortunately, I routinely got targeted as one of these subjects.

It did not take long to ascertain that others were also having serious problems with this newcomer. Some of the medical center's most dedicated volunteers wanted nothing to do with her and came directly to me instead. Several even threatened to quit. This further inflamed her animosity toward me and led to accusations of undermining authority. She especially alienated several service groups, one of which was a veterans' organization that routinely drove 120 miles round-trip to donate magazines and books. I still remember the representative of this organization seething after my boss instructed him that their long-standing contributions were no longer needed.

To diffuse the situation and the potential fallout, I met with my boss over this predicament. She flatly retorted there were more than enough reading materials for our patients. I then explained to her that Jerry had previously arranged with these donors to provide any excess magazines, such as *National Geographic* and *Smithsonian*, to the school district warehouse. Hearing this, she immediately went ballistic and threatened to file charges relating to the improper disposal of federal property. According to her policy interpretation, all excess magazines and books need to be tossed into the dumpster.

Ranting about Jerry's past ways of doing things, she mandated that everything would now go strictly by the book. Although I wanted to snap back that her book was the only one belonging in the trash bin, venturing any deeper into the doghouse was not advisable.

As another show of authority, this gal had one of the storage areas emptied out. Into the dumpster went old movie equipment and a vintage collection of 8mm reels. Dating back to the late 1940's, these films contributed to the recreational therapy activities for hospitalized veterans. Also cleared out were cases of playing cards and other novelties donated by the area casinos. Other items now gone as well included the Christmas tree lights used each year to decorate a giant spruce tree, trucked in from the Sierras and set up by the Lake Almanor Elks Club.

A few weeks after my boss's melee over magazine donations, the school district notified me that our medical center would be receiving their annual community service award for our contributions to the Crayons to Computers warehouse. When my boss learned of this award, she replaced me and attended the ceremony to personally accept the commendation. This then served as hypocrisy by the book.

Again, I was not the only one being ticked off by this bitter critter of a boss. She continually berated Jerry's past practices for not following federal policy. Certain volunteers brought on board by Jerry, seemed viewed as rift-raft by this lady. Many left as she began cleaning house. Although a fair number of volunteers complained to the medical center director, he often dismissed the concerns by claiming that I was vindictively behind their grievances and undermining this supervisor, whom he had personally selected and fully supported.

From the very beginning, my new boss evoked frustration over the computerized office system that Jerry had implemented in this department. During the interview process, this lady boasted of considerable computer proficiency and thus earned a higher score than me on this rating credential. Several days after coming on board, my new supervisor asked me for records regarding the volunteer program. After handing her the floppy disks, a flustered reaction followed. When I asked as to whether she knew how to use these disks, my boss just replied that regular computer use was not a requirement at her last job. Further on, her lack of computer skills, as compared to mine, became more evident. As such, more red flags began rising, and the friction between us heightened. Looming in the background was also that EEO complaint that I had filed. Little by little, this complaint was gaining increased credibility, and she begrudgingly seemed to sense it.

Throughout her tenure, my boss's behavior kept treading toward bizarre. One of the saddest events to happen on the job occurred when she booted out a cognitively impaired volunteer. This dedicated individual had spent several years assisting our patients and staff while bolstering his own self-image. Although there were times when his language became vulgar, most of us learned to understand that this conduct stemmed from his disabling condition and, therefore, was by no means blatantly abusive behavior. When my supervisor got wind of this situation, she immediately banned the young man from continuing as a volunteer. Following the haphazard dismissal, I encountered this individual sitting outside the medical center in his wheelchair. While awaiting the paratransit van to pick him up, he shared with me what had transpired. Devastated by this ordeal and the loss of his most important social connection, this former contributor sat broken with his head hung down. Neither of us understood what had precipitated his being singled out just now for such drastic action. There were staff and many patients at this place whose crusty language far exceeded the impact of this particular volunteer's vocabulary.

Based on this incident, I was almost certain that a cantankerous coot named Gene would be the next to go. From the hat that topped off his balding crown, to the roper boots that grounded him, Gene was a tried and true cowboy, the real McCoy. Aside from a WWII stint as a U.S. Army muleskinner, he rode the western range throughout most of his younger years. Gene's only wartime injury came from a nasty kick to the side of his right leg. This confrontation left Gene with a bum leg. Some say that it also embedded in Gene a personality similar to the animal which had kicked him. Nonetheless, he loyally volunteered endless hours hobbling about the medical center. While doing so, his routine cussing sounded as if he were still driving cattle. Because of his work ethic, Gene's contributions earned him a volunteer of the year commendation.

Most of us had become accustomed to Gene's crusty nature, yet every so often, there would be complaints about his refrains. In an effort to tone done his Wild-West lingo, I met with Gene one day to discuss this situation. As usual, Gene responded with the tough character façade. Although this was nothing more than a game of charades, I knew to proceed with caution. When dealing with someone who has weathered six marriages and an untold number of cattle drives, you tread carefully. Midway through our conversation, however, Gene surprised me with a humbled confession that he was losing his hearing. As such, this contrite cattleman noted that he often responds to others in a surly fashion, simply because, he no longer hears a lot of what is being said to him. Knowing that confessions don't come easy for old wranglers like Gene, something had to be done about this travesty.

At times, turnabouts come when you least expect them. The following day I stopped by the office of the MD in charge of the outpatient clinic. After sharing with this physician my concern about Gene's hearing loss, Dr. Kurt demonstrated to me one of the most caring considerations I had ever encountered in this highly bureaucratic system. After explaining to me that Gene's veteran status did not allow eligibility for outpatient audiology services, Dr. Kurt applied ingenuity and improvised. According to the VA rules, the only way Gene's hearing problem could be addressed is by discovering it during an inpatient stay. Therefore, Gene's bum leg suddenly required him to be hospitalized. During his stay, a coincidental diagnosis determined that Gene needed and would get hearing aids. This was done because Dr. Kurt truly appreciated the volunteer work he often observed being done by this vintage saddle tramp.

Instead of Gene, my boss's next target became a volunteer named Walt. I will be the first to admit that this guy could be all too goofy, exceedingly quirky, and even annoying at times. His Gomer Pyle impersonations became a personal trademark. I guess you could call Walt the Beetle Bailey of this place. Once you got past the eccentric personality, however, you came to know a lovable volunteer with over thirty-five thousand hours of service at this medical center. He pushed the wheelchairs, delivered medical charts, visited patients, provided rides, picked up the donated bakery goods, gave tours, manned the information desk, assisted the chaplain, and joined me every so often for a Whopper and fries at Burger King. Despite battling serious maladies of his own, this guy was the salt of the earth when it came to helping fellow disabled veterans. After my boss hinted about getting rid of Walt, I went on the offense and nominated him for a prestigious national award from the Disabled American Veterans organization. He earned, deserved, and won this honor. To say the least, my belligerent boss blew her top and acted madder than a hatter.

Several weeks later, I received a lifetime achievement award, which pertained to activities outside of my workplace. When my picture and an accompanying story got featured in the local newspaper, instead of any congratulations, my boss threatened to reprimand me for not obtaining her prior permission and approval for this accolade. Without a doubt, this perturbed lady seemed hell-bent on finding fault with everything.

To deal with the antics of my boss, I had the shoulder of a cherished confidant to lean on. Major Ralph was a survivor of the infamous Bataan Death March. Having been a prisoner of war during this horrific WWII episode, Ralph knew how to deal with any and all adversity. As a volunteer, this dedicated veteran assisted other ex-POW's with their VA benefits. Because his work was so highly regarded by the VA, Ralph had his own private office and phone at this medical center. From his interactions with my boss, he did not have a favorable opinion of this lady. Ralph once joked to me that I was a prisoner of war in this gal's battlefield. I really do not know what I would have done without this sage soldier as a sounding board. Like Walt, I helped to nominate Ralph for a national award. As a result, Ralph got flown to Constitution Hall in Washington, D.C., where he received the DAR's top commendation for services to America's veterans. He remains one of the most impressive individuals I have ever met.

When the medical center began undergoing major renovations, the voluntary service and public affairs offices relocated to an upper floor. Although this placed our department in a more out of the way setting, we gained in square footage. My boss somehow viewed this departmental relocation as a personal affront. She seemed to want control over everything and insisted that her new office space be completely remodeled. Antagonized by her constant grumbling, the maintenance staff finally complied with her wishes by repainting the room and carpeting the tile floor with leftover remnant pieces. Along with this patchwork floor covering, her office now sported freshly painted orange walls. Upon inspecting the updated enclave, my boss freaked out. Whether viable or not, she claimed to have a physical aversion to the color orange. The oddball carpet pattern only added to her despair. However, the maintenance staff did not have the time or resources to make any further changes. According to them, she got what she asked for. Meanwhile, I was more than satisfied with my modest corner office and a private entrance, which allowed more frequent escapes from the tyranny.

During this transition, the ongoing fury of my boss seemed to be escalating. Rather than just complaining about me or the volunteers, her commentary switched to chastising upper management. Uncharacteristically, she even consulted me about some administrative issues. Whatever was eating away at this lady, had built up to an explosive level. Therefore, the next eventful happening more than lit her fuse. After just a short time in this new office arrangement, administration announced that I would be transferred to a new position under the supervision of the associate medical center director. Caught totally off-guard by this rigmarole, my now former boss stormed into my office and confronted me. To say the least, she was fuming and fit to be tied. Then things got really weird.

A number of workdays went by without any further episodes or confrontations. Regular visits from the volunteers kept me tuned in to the rumor mill. Out of the blue, however, an announcement suddenly surfaced that my former boss had broken her ankle and would be out of her office for an unspecified time. As an ironic result, I then got directed to temporarily cover her absence. This meant I would now occupy two offices. Although administration noted to me that this lady had reportedly slipped on a wet floor near the hospital entrance, two volunteers clued me in on a different take. Both of them claimed to have seen her scurrying erratically down a corridor and mumbling to herself. All of a sudden, she snagged one foot on the other. By doing so, this gal tripped herself and fell awkwardly to the ground. They also mentioned hearing numerous obscenities, which I cannot repeat.

After learning that this lady was now on crutches, I had yet to see her since this incident. Less than a week following her injury, I showed up for work one morning and was hastily confronted by the office secretary, Mary. She insisted that

I immediately come with her and look inside the glowing orange office of my former boss. I did and was amazed. The entire office had been cleared of all her belongings. Nothing remained, except a desk, bookshelf, some office supplies, and, of course, that funky carpet. Since she left for her sick leave, nobody in the building recalled seeing anyone go in or out of this gal's office. All we could surmise was that she clandestinely hobbled in during the wee hours of the night and removed her personal possessions. But why the secretive approach, we wondered. The medical center director wondered as well and began calling me to ask of her whereabouts. I could only answer honestly that I had no idea. However, I did relish the circumstances that the director's choice to run the voluntary services department, instead of me, had now vanished into thin air. This moment of vindication again reminded me, that what goes around, comes around.

Nevermore and never again did this eccentric supervisor appear at the Reno VA Medical Center. As such, the rumors ran amuck. One of the stories claimed that I had her kidnapped and left out in the desolate Nevada desert. Someone else said she had been spotted in Arizona. Others claimed this lady now resided in the casinos. The seedy grapevine cultivated a lot of fruit to feast upon.

Lasting less than a year, my combatant boss had flown out of the cuckoo's nest and winged off to a location unknown. Somehow, it did not matter where as long as there was no return migration. As for me, I remained in this crazy nest and got temporarily promoted as the chief birdbrain. Down the line, however, cuckoo times would constantly resurface. And just in case you are curious about that EEOC complaint and investigation, it finally got settled. Like so many government maneuverings, the details remain classified and clandestine.

The Godbrother

Without Wiley Coyotes around, no Road Runners would ever be up to speed.

L ester was my friend, the mobster, at least I think so. After first meeting this mysterious guy, I had no idea that a contract had been taken out on me. Fortunately, the contract represented a pledge of protection by Lester. And like it or not, he thus became my godbrother.

Working at the VA medical center in Reno, it was by no means unusual to have characters like Lester suddenly show up and sign on as a volunteer. Before I even got to know anything about this guy, my eccentric newcomer boss assigned him to assist the voluntary services office. From that moment forward, Lester took charge.

Some people have a knack for assessing others. This certainly was Lester's forte. It did not take him long to size me up. After learning about these faulty headlights of mine, Lester declared himself my guide dog, guard dog, and watchdog. These roles came naturally to Lester, who had a pit bull demeanor, pug stature, and the heart of a St. Bernard. Lester was a protector, most of which stemmed from his background in the Marine Corps. It was never hard to tell that he had been a leatherneck and devil dog. To him, I was like a wounded marine buddy. This, however, was not a matter of sympathy but, more like loyalty. I had become his comrade and no one dared to harm me. Manning the desk just outside my office entrance, Lester screened everyone before allowing them to approach further.

Having what now amounted to a personal bodyguard was extremely uncustomary to me. Usually, battles were fought on my own. Although there were times when I relied on a little help from my friends, nothing matched the caliber of Lester's intervention and domineering personality.

As a volunteer at this medical center, Lester's job involved signing in the volunteers, monitoring their hours, greeting visitors, distributing meal vouchers, and answering phones. The desk he manned was located adjacent to my office. His work schedule generally encompassed two to three days a week.

From the very start, Lester became an instant curiosity. Due to his lifestyle and storied past, many wondered why this stylish high-roller chose to volunteer. Nonetheless, he took every assignment seriously, while questions kept circulating as to who this character is and why he is here? Admittedly, I often leaned toward the same inquisitions.

This veterans' medical center had hundreds of active volunteers, both young and old, who contributed for varying reasons. Many represented retirees lending their skills and experiences. Some were just plain lonely and needed to socialize. Still, there were those who had faced adversity and wanted to share in a positive exchange. What they all had in common was a desire to honor and serve our nation's military veterans.

Despite interacting with volunteers from all walks of life, I had yet to ever meet anyone quite like Lester. The more I learned about him, the more intrigued I became. Lester never bragged directly about his background, but hinted profusely. Raised by a single parent, who Lester described as mentally impaired and dysfunctional, he grew up on the streets of New York City. He also mentioned having a son institutionalized in Southern California with a diagnosis similar to that of his mother's.

Lester's tales about growing up on the NYC mean streets were nothing short of entertaining. He recalled routinely jumping from the rooftops of one high-rise to another. For an even greater test of daring, Lester and his friends would lie between the subway rails as the train passed over them. And just to further prove themselves as tough guys, they chewed on tar extracted from the hot summer streets. Lester's tales of Marine Corps training were equally mind-boggling. He shared many intriguing details of military discipline.

Even though notably far-fetched, contesting Lester's stories would not be wise, especially those advocating mobster ties. According to Lester, shortly after his military stint, he returned to work in New York City as a carpet installer. This involved being employed by his uncle. Many clients of this family- owned business were celebrities with connections. This eventually led to Lester meeting shady characters in high places. As such, he eventually got offered a Las Vegas job during its mobster-influenced heydays. Lester touted his southern Nevada career as the floor manager for a major casino. From Lester's description, this lucrative lookout job entailed watching and listening to whatever conspired on the premises. Other obligations required him to occasionally sign various papers with no questions asked. One of the recollections shared by Lester was seeing certain clientele being escorted to the head honcho's office. A short time later, someone would approach this same office with a large laundry cart, roll it quickly inside, and exit thereafter with the same cart now loaded. However, neither hide nor hair of the clientele would be seen again. Strange things did happen in this era.

Because Lester was a person of contrasts, it was hard to second-guess his renditions. He routinely showed up dressed to the hilt. Although he did forego a necktie, a tailored blazer, dress slacks, and shiny wingtips represented his standard attire. Lester's always closely-cropped haircut was military issue. Prim and proper, a clean-shaven face never showcased any signs of stubble or five o'clock shadow. To the best of my recollection, I also recall something like a Rolex garnished his wrist.

Lester definitely had a tough guy persona. His boxing-ring nose appeared somewhat flattened from repeated punches. The bags under both eyes emphasized his restlessness. Cocking his head to one side and staring intently, even this character's posture hinted of intimidation.

According to my sources, Lester lived in a modest home, where he stored both a Lincoln and a Mercedes. Claiming to be bored with the Mercedes, he impulsively sold it one day for a fraction of its value. It was not unusual for Lester to walk into the medical center with gifts for the staff and volunteers. Sometimes, it was clothing, other times jewelry, and, of course, there was that awkward episode when I got called to the VAMC director's office because Lester was handing out $100 bills. Upon learning that nursing staff hours were being reduced due to budget cuts, he stood at one of the ward stations and offered $100 to any employee needing assistance. By the time I caught up with Lester and diverted him away from the mayhem, he had already allegedly given out $1200 in cash.

There was also an occasion when a fellow volunteer, a former marine as well, noted to Lester how much he wished he had a dress uniform to wear in area parades. The next week, Lester booked two seats on a jet to San Diego, where he then escorted this friend to Camp Pendleton and bought him a $400 Marine Corps uniform. After returning, Lester befriended another former marine and volunteer, who often got referred to as Chicago Joe. When Lester discovered that this guy was destitute and essentially living on the streets of Reno, he took Joe downtown and bought him new clothes, so that no one would complain about Joe's shabby coverings while volunteering.

A comical sideline to Lester's antics came from his interactions with my crackerjack secretary, Mary. Although tolerant and understanding, Mary never quite got used to Lester's imposing personality. The two had an ongoing heated exchange. Each morning as Mary entered the office, she would crank open the windows and turn on the fan to cool things down. After Lester's later morning arrival, he then methodically closed the windows and shut down the fan to raise the temperature. I guess warmhearted Mary could not accept that cold-blooded mobsters like it hot.

Sometimes Lester would catch you off guard with his invitations and generosity. At the end of one workday, he announced to me and several others that, along with our spouses, we needed to join him and his wife for supper at the Hilton. After mentioning to him that I must first arrange for a babysitter, Lester ominously snapped back that attendance was mandatory at this dining event. That's the way Lester approached these matters. Hastily acquiring a babysitter, Dianna and I indeed showed up to join three other couples. Seated next to Lester, he suddenly nudged me during the meal and said that he wanted to show me something I probably had never seen before. Reaching into his blazer pocket, Lester pulled out a micro handgun. In a subdued voice, he proudly proclaimed, "It's the worlds' smallest pistol." Staring at the outline of the miniature weapon in the palm of his hand, I had no response to this predicament. All I could think about at the moment was this town's notorious taboo against any firearm in a casino. However, I was in no position to challenge Lester's judgment or possession.

The surprises did not end here. Just as we finished our meals, Lester instructed everyone to head for the slot machines. With that, he next handed several rolls of $1 tokens to each of us. While some in this party hesitated, Lester sternly reminded us that acceptance of the offer was not optional. He then directed us to a specific row of one-armed bandits. I tried assessing the reaction of Lester's wife, Sidney, to his handing out a small fortune and footing the bill for the entire supper tab, she neither commented nor flinched. As far as I know, no one hit any jackpots on this night. As usual, the casino had the upper hand when it came to deposits and returns. Therefore, none of us left richer than when we arrived.

Not long after this social night, I began to see changes

in Lester's behavior. He was becoming more agitated and demanding about everything around him. In the months before, he generally wavered back and forth from mellow to madcap. One day Lester showed up with two brand new turtlenecks in hand, one black and the other white. He then presented them to me and asked which one I would like. Although feeling uneasy about accepting any gifts from him, I knew better than to contest any offer. As such, I pointed to the black one and instantly found Lester enraged that I had not picked the white one. He then turned and stormed out of the office. During the next couple of weeks, there had been various reports to me about likewise exchanges with Lester. Perhaps the most awkward was being summoned to the medical center director's office because of a demand made by Lester. Maintaining his guard dog demeanor, Lester decided to confront the director and tell him that I deserved a promotion. Lester then followed up by threatening to withhold a major donation to the medical center if this did not occur. Upon my arrival to his office, the irate VAMC director wanted to know why I had put Lester up to this coercion. This was a difficult position for me. While not wanting to take sides against Lester, I did not favor being credited for his eccentric conduct. Most of all, I really liked the guy and feared seeing him branded negatively. However, the whacky situations continued to accelerate.

Again, doubting Lester seemed fraught with risks. Was he really a former mobster? Did he have underworld ties? Was the Nevada constable badge he sometimes flashed, even legitimate? Could this guy be dangerous? To answer these questions, I actually had a friend check with contacts in Las Vegas. It turned out that Lester's family name was indeed connected to one of the most sinister gaming syndicates during the mobster days. However, there seemed to have been a falling out between Lester and his kin at some point. As a rule of caution, it is not a good idea to dig too deeply into such matters. From what I found out, Lester was indeed associated with the shady side of

Las Vegas. There appeared to be a genuine possibility of his stories having merit. My conclusion is that Lester's past life did have some involvement without notoriety in the mobster world. I really suspected that Lester could not disclose everything yet desperately wanted some credit for being part of the epic Nevada gaming era. Therefore, he needed to be distinguished as more than just some nobody street kid from New York City.

During this period of Lester's increased edginess, the incidents grew stranger and stranger. Whether it was meant to impress me or caution me, Lester freaked me out with an invitation to accompany him on a weekend trip to Italy. He noted that he had some urgent business to take care of and that I should join him. At this point I wanted to agree and, thus, call what I thought was a bluff. Something inside me, however, said that if I were to accept this invitation, I might actually find myself airborne to lasagna land. I just had to gracefully decline.

Perhaps my scariest moment came the Friday morning when Lester began bragging about the automatic weapons in his car trunk. This was federal property and by no means did I desire dealing with any arsenal in Lester's vehicle. At this moment, I again recalled the pip-squeak pistol he had previously revealed at the casino. Whether it was right or wrong, I reverted to a Sgt. Schultz mode. Like this German television character from *Hogan's Heroes*, I wanted to know nothing. However, my stomach and morals became unsettled. Was this just bravado by Lester or something more serious? Had he gone off the deep end, or did this just represent business as usual? Before I could make any assessment, Lester simply disappeared for the rest of the day.

At this juncture, I should digress by disclosing that Lester was not my first encounter with firepower at this medical center. While collecting items for the Military Heritage Museum, the widow of a WWI veteran dropped off a box of his wartime memorabilia. After pulling out uniforms and patches, at the bottom of this container lay an authentic Howitzer shell. Of course it had to be a dud, right? Just to be on the safe side, I called a nearby military base and inquired on how to assess this historical gem. Within the hour, chaos ensued as my office got stormed by a U.S. Army bomb squad. Fortunately, a munitions expert certified the shell as harmless. Better to be safe than sorry, I guess.

It would be remiss if I did not also recount the day when an authentic WWII torpedo landed just outside the nursing home ward of this medical center. A dedicated navy veteran nicknamed "Bay Leaves", crusaded to erect a memorial to fellow submariners and targeted the Reno VAMC grounds as the perfect site. This passionate navy man paid a major portion of his lifesavings to have this torpedo shipped here by rail from Seattle and crane-mounted onto concrete footings. He even commissioned students at a local industrial arts school to forge an iron submarine scale replica and affix it to the top of this torpedo.

In contrast to the opinion of the VAMC director, I viewed this exterior memorial as a compliment to the nearby interior museum. Because of a bureaucratic debacle, the sky-blue torpedo eventually ended up being launched over to the State Veterans Cemetery. Considering this misguided torpedo, the Howitzer blowup, and now Lester's loaded accounts, my job entailed some potentially explosive moments.

Following Lester's weapon revelation on Friday, I cherished my weekend away from work. As this respite culminated, the TV got turned on to watch the Sunday evening local news. My weekend was about to end in the same mode it had begun. The broadcast began by announcing that a man had just been arrested while brandishing a gun within one of the casinos. Just as the picture was flashed and his name announced, I moved closer to the TV screen. I then sat there gawking at a mug shot of my buddy Lester. As a result of this incident,

Lester ended up behind bars. During his incarceration, he threatened the law enforcement authorities, fired his lawyer, and barred visits from any friends. Too afraid and unsettled to contact him, I complied with his wishes. Unfortunately, I would never see Lester again.

During the times when Lester's strange behavior began escalating, I found out he had been undergoing frequent medical care. Lester always put up a brave face and never wanted anyone to see him as vulnerable. Even as a well-trained former marine, there were certain fights which he could not win. The one called pancreatic cancer was just such a battle. Due to this disease and its toxic treatment, Lester was slowly losing control of the world around him. Before the entire tale had yet to be told, his storied life was coming to an end. Lester had earned recognition for others, without creating a name for himself. I believe this bothered him more than anything else. Then again, perhaps all the secrets he hinted about were just make-believe fables. Nonetheless, this squirrelly character often served as a Rocky in the midst of Bullwinkle moments. In doing so, Lester lived to rescue those around him.

Maybe my friend, the mobster, was never really a mobster at all. It doesn't matter to me. Whether Lester personified a godbrother or not, he became my guide dog, guard dog, and watchdog, which is just the way I will remember him. Should any reminder be further needed, atop my bookshelf is the fuzzy Wiley Coyote toy that Lester gave to my daughter, Brianna. This cartoon character is so much like Lester, always anxious and entertaining in every episode.

And for the record, none of what has been cautiously exposed should ever give credence to the malicious rumor that I personally hired Lester to kidnap a certain former adversarial boss of mine and leave her hopelessly stranded in the deadly Nevada desert.

The Emperor's Old Clothes

A book can indeed be judged by its cover, once you have looked inside and read between the lines.

Somewhere out there is a man meandering about in giant pants. There is simply no mistaking this audacious guy. His name is Frank, and he is an extraordinary street musician. If you happen to see him, please let Frank know that I am still searching for that French horn he so desperately desires.

With my departure from Reno, I left behind the Sierras and trekked into the Cascades. This third Wild-West rendezvous landed me in the boomtown of Bend, Oregon. Instead of a gaming town with high stakes and high rollers, this new homeland was a recreational Mecca of ski slopes, canyon climbs, trout holes, whitewater navigating, and bike trails. When I first discovered this place in the late 1980's, it housed just over fourteen thousand residents. By the late '90s, Bend exceeded fifty thousand and was growing. Therefore, my family and I were not the only ones migrating here. Like past locations, this new transition held the promise of a new career, added adventures, and some incredibly interesting characters. Frank touched upon all three.

When I first met Frank, he appeared at the doorway to the office where I now worked as a mediator and outreach coordinator for an Oregon dispute resolution agency. If Frank's arrival sounds like a recurring theme, it is. Just about every job I have started has attracted an odd encounter within the first few days of work. This time, however, the character in my doorway was neither a Santa Claus nor Hamm with hides. Instead, this wayfarer, now towering before me, reigned as a rogue nobleman in the strangest suit of armor.

Frank's crown of bushy hair barely cleared the entrance, while his shoulders filled the entire frame. This character's height, width, and dark bewhiskered face created a domineering figure. Frank's physical features, however, paled in comparison to his outlandish attire, especially the giant pants that enveloped his lower extremities. In fact, the word *giant* is totally inadequate. Frank wore pants that were gargantuan, behemoth, and downright leviathan as leggings.

Throwbacks from the hippie days, Frank's britches would have been dubbed far-out by those on the far side. These were not simply Beatles-era bell bottoms but what was once referred to as elephant bells. In this particular case, they represented the entire pachyderm herd. Oftentimes, a sheepskin vest accented this outfit. Based on his hairy features, burly stature, and these dinosaur dungarees, Frank could have easily performed under the catchy stage name of Wooly Mammoth.

I have no idea where or how Frank acquired these jumbo jeans, yet each faded denim leg resembled a wrap skirt from the knees on down. At the very least, these leggings flared out to a diameter exceeding two feet wide. As they brushed along the floor, they virtually swept aside everything in their path. Whenever standing on a street corner, Frank often resembled a human weather vane, whose pants' legs flapped like schooner sails while indicating the direction and intensity of any prevailing winds. If not for Frank being such a big man, a blustery day would have sent him hang-gliding. From the very first time I became acquainted with this local curiosity, these pants were his one and only bottom-half ensemble.

Although I was fairly new to this central Oregon community, I had encountered Frank several times in the midst of his sidewalk musical sessions. Because of my past history of being drawn to quirky folks like him, destiny seemed to mandate that our paths would eventually cross. Now in my new career as a dispute resolution mediator, my experiences would encompass interacting with more than a fair share of this community's resident characters.

Frank came to my workplace searching for justice and a French horn. When the van in which he homesteaded broke down and got towed to a local repair shop, it ended up in a different kind of fix. Somehow this van caught fire at the shop, and as a result, Frank lost most everything he owned. This included a cherished French horn stored inside his vehicle. Somehow Frank managed to get a settlement to replace his incinerated van, charred clothes, and flamed-out acoustic guitar. According to Frank, however, no concessions were made for the horn that melted down in this melee. It was a prized possession he never stopped thinking about. Without this melodic instrument, Frank could not be whole. He was owed another French horn, and yet nothing was being done.

About the only other cherished possession that Frank owned was a midsized mongrel named Spike. Together, the two were inseparable. Both shared the replacement van that now served as their mobile home. Therefore, wherever Frank ventured, Spike did likewise.

As a wandering minstrel who spent his days crooning from roadsides and store fronts, Frank appeared content with his lifestyle. The only thing missing from his daily existence was that French horn, whose loss he continually grieved. Frank was adamant that the fire settlement had been an injustice for not replacing his French fried horn. The loss of this sentimental horn seemed to consume Frank each and every day. Something had to be done, and that is why Frank sought out my assistance. Conversations with Frank were nothing less than entertaining. Aside from his dispute, he had many items to jawbone over. It was not unusual for Frank to jump from one thing to another. Oftentimes, you were especially grateful that he did.

After unloading the details of his fire settlement, it became apparent that Frank had already signed a binding agreement, which left him with little, if any, recourse. Explaining this to

Frank was difficult. As much as I wanted to help the guy, this dilemma seemed at an impasse. When Frank switched the subject to talk about his guitar strumming, I quickly accepted the changeover and shared with him my similar six-string past. That became the only cue Frank needed to hear. He instantly left my office and returned moments later with the most deplorable music maker I had ever laid eyes upon. This guitar was shamelessly painted flat blue and marred by several holes punched through its wooden top. Frank stated that he had another guitar, yet favored this one because it had been homeless and rescued by him from a dumpster. With this now said, Frank then began finger-picking and singing. Once he started playing, Frank required no audience approval or further prompting. In a world all his own, he surrounded himself in the music. As I listened, it did not take long to realize the talent and creativity of this artist. Frank's enormous fingers danced across the strings while his deep gravelly voice followed in step. He did not belong on the streets but should be showcased on a main stage. For Frank, however, that would have been like trying to fit him into a dress suit.

After remarking to Frank that he should be performing at paying venues, his response caught me off guard. Frank stated that he wouldn't do so because most places won't allow Spike to accompany him. He simply valued the dog's friendship more than any material gains. As such, his lifestyle was one of choice, which unfortunately offended others. During one street curb performance, Frank recalled how a police officer ordered him to leave and then kicked over his guitar case. The few sparse donations tossed into this case, were then spilled out onto the road. Frank often got the boot because of his stigma as a street person. Those with little time to listen and even lesser capacity for compassion were all too anxious to overreact to this guy's mystique and way of life.

As best as I tried to understand Frank's French horn issue, nothing could be worked out. Nonetheless, Frank continued to stop by my office on a regular basis. For many others, that would have been unacceptable. Frank's stature and unorthodox appearance scared a lot of people. His equally imposing aroma, stemming from too many days without a shower, also created an interesting challenge. At times I had to hold my breath and put understanding ahead of olfactory annoyance. This same measure often became necessary during prior encounters with homeless veterans.

When I learned that Frank was a Vietnam-era veteran and had been discharged due to a diagnosis of schizophrenia, my past outreach work with disabled veterans reminded me that this military man deserved more than just my time. He was due a greater appreciation and some federal VA benefits. Like so many vets from this wartime era, however, Frank wanted nothing to do with a bureaucracy of endless paperwork and evaluations. All he really needed was that French horn.

My interest in Frank can be directly blamed on three other Vietnam-era veterans. Jim, Clair, and David were professional advocates. Like me, Jim and Clare worked for the U.S. Department of Veterans Affairs, while David operated a private sector disability rights agency. As an outreach specialist, Jim concentrated on assisting homeless and Native American veterans. Despite battling injuries from a paratrooper episode, Jim's endless humanitarian efforts to help fellow veterans earned him national recognition. Several times a year, Jim would drive from Seattle to the Walla Walla VA Medical Center and then accompany me on outreach excursions. Together we combed the countryside for connections with underserved veterans. A lot of this work led us to area reservations and a cultural education.

In reaching out to veterans, Clair vastly contrasted Jim's dress-suit style and approach yet embodied the same dedication. Clair showcased a gruff personality that appeared to stem from Agent Orange and other war-related experiences. He served a regional area around Yakima, where he oftentimes grumbled as much about the government as the veterans he assisted. As a result, Clare tended to butt heads with the bureaucracy. All too often, however, I agreed with his perspective, which sometimes landed both of us in hot water.

David was a blend of both Jim and Clair. Upon his return from Vietnam, David and his fiance took a cruise up the scenic Geiger Grade, just outside Carson City, Nevada. Forced off the road by a reckless driver, a horrific crash took the life of David's fiance and left him paralyzed from the waist on down. Through resilience, David overcame this tragedy to become an acclaimed advocate for those challenged by adversity. I met him when the two of us were appointed to the Governor's ADA Council. While raising hackles and awareness, David created a burgeoning consulting business called Barrier Free Design. When it came to championing disability rights, David challenged Goliath by changing many entrenched attitudes. Pulled about in his wheelchair by a Doberman named Pepper, David enhanced the lives of people throughout Nevada and the surrounding states.

What I admired most about Jim, Clair, and David was that each shared the same passions and perseverance to lend a helping hand. Each of them became a role model for me. As such, I always tried to follow in their footsteps. This trio improved my acuity to see Frank and others from different viewpoints.

Having dealt with adversity myself, perhaps that is another reason why I empathized with Frank. Then again, maybe it was just a mutual love of six-string acoustics. It might even have been the fact that Frank was one of the few persons I could actually identify from a distance. Those humungous leggings, slapping against one another as he walked, could always be recognized from far, far away.

After just a couple of years in my mediator role and attempting to resolve all kinds of antagonisms, family ties required that I uproot and return to my home state. This career as a mediator was intriguing and something I anticipated continuing. My favorite experience remains to be that custody case involving a pet cat. Also fascinating was the dispute in which a new home owner decided to enhance his mountain view by chain-sawing off the tops of his neighbor's spruce trees. Writing a newspaper advice column called *Mending Fences* proved to be interesting as well, especially the phone call it evoked from an elderly lady. She apparently misunderstood the column's moniker and requested me to repair her broken front yard gate.

Because of my move back to Northern Wisconsin, it now has been years since last seeing melodious Frank. I'm sure he is still strumming away in a downtown location, where some listeners marvel at his artistry, while others only judge him by his cover. To some of us, Frank is a constant and uncomfortable reminder of what happens to many veterans following their service to this country. In many ways, Frank still battles as a soldier but, this time, fights a lifelong adversary that others often misunderstand. I really miss the guy and wish him well. Even more so, I desperately hope he gets that French horn someday. It is just too bad my friend Lester is no longer still around. Just one call to him and Frank would again be blowing his own horn. However, Lester's insistence to also outfit Frank in new clothes would never suit this emperor of street strumming and serenades.

The Ugliest Duckling

If it walks like an ugly duck and talks like an ugly duck, it most likely will never become a beautiful swan.

Not every ugly duckling turns into an elegant swan. Most just remain run-of-the-mill ducks. However, there are a few that transform into the foulest of fowl. Unfortunately, I had an unsettling encounter with one of them. As a result, a whole lot of feathers got vigorously ruffled. And of course, there was what you might call "quacklash" as well.

While residing in Central Oregon, my conscience began urging me to reach out more and help others facing challenges similar to mine. At this same time, a national disability and advocacy organization coincidentally held a community meeting to charter a local chapter. Adhering to what seemed like an omen, I showed up at this gathering.

Specifically, this organization represented blind and visually impaired individuals. It had a network of chapters in every state. Although I had previously interacted with a number of nonprofit associations, this was my first introduction to a group totally dedicated to my particular circumstances. When the attendees of this meeting agreed to form a local chapter, I signed on and soon found myself serving as one of its elected officers. Just a few months later, I then got appointed to this organization's state board of directors. As a result, I now found myself parked alongside all kinds of faulty headlights. What lay ahead were driving lessons like never before.

In the beginning, my membership cultivated a lot of new friendships. This involvement gave me an opportunity to share triumphs, tribulations, and possibly some advice. What I had not expected, however, was that my headlights would shine on some unsavory escapades.

From past experiences of mine, one of the best ways to deal with your own personal adversity is to assist others with theirs. I anxiously jumped into this new venture, hoping to do just that. At the same time, I was not opposed to any healthy exchanges that might benefit me. Due to my career background of investigating issues and reviewing reports, it may not have been such a good idea to quickly include me on this organization's state board. My inquisitive nature got triggered immediately. Following the first meeting at this level, things started smelling fishy. After examining the treasurer's report, I noticed a huge sum of money being diverted to a contracted private sector fundraiser. Of the monies raised in a statewide campaign, the fundraiser retained over seventy percent of the donations. Upon inquiring about this, the response back to me was that this ratio was standard practice in the fundraising arena. Based on the prior nonprofit boards I had served on, this answer did not agree with me. Knowing that many of this organization's members were unemployed, I then queried as to why these folks are not being hired and trained to conduct the fundraising calls. The perplexing answer was that the members generally lacked the professionalism needed in this activity. Again, this did not jive with my experiences. What I eventually ended up discovering were some questionable personal ties between the state president and the fundraiser.

Another rude awakening came when this organization flew me cross-country to Washington D.C for its annual lobbying seminar. This forum involved both a general orientation on current issues and personal visits to congressional offices. Before assembling with my state contingent for the legislative tour, the Oregon state president approached me and displayed two white canes. Like me, this gal had Stargardt's. Utilizing her peripheral acuity, she meandered about without the white canes and guide dogs used by most of the members. To my surprise, this state president now held out a white cane and told me that I would need it. When I responded back that I never use a cane, she concurred, but told me that my using one while meeting with the legislators would create a more credible impression. Taken back by this charade, my next expectation was to be handed a pair of dark glasses. I instantly felt like this entire event was nothing more than a mission of mercy. By no means could I accept any prop and begin a masquerade. My entire aim for joining in this effort was to demonstrate the different ways each of us adapts. I wanted to exemplify as well that not all faulty headlights are completely shorted out. It now became more than evident that it was not just the legislators who needed greater educating. This lobbying venue opened my eyes to one of the major reasons why so many individuals choose not to join certain advocacy organizations.

Several months later, I got sponsored to attend this organization's national convention in Atlanta. Among the organized melee of members with white canes and guide dogs, there were also individuals like me without these modes of guidance. What really caught my eye, however, was witnessing the personal entourage that accompanied the Oregon state president at this event. Using chapter funds, she sponsored her mother, daughter, and husband. I believe she had a son there as well. Also present was her colleague from the private Montessori school, where this state president worked. The only missing relative from this kindred junket, seemed to be her father, who she had put in charge of the chapter's accounting and recordkeeping.

Because of my partial acuity, I was one of the few to actually see this tomfoolery. When I asked the state president to explain this situation, she laughed it off by saying that sighted volunteers were routinely needed. By no means did this set well with me. As the convention continued on, things got even stranger. At one of the general sessions, small-scale statues were handed out to all the conventioneers. These miniature metal busts represented someone who the organization appeared to religiously revere as their patron saint. To me, this seemed just plain weird. I felt like I was being handed a Buddha and now needed to rub his belly. During this same session, a speaker from the media giant CNN, talked to the group about how this news network covers health issues. Following this formal presentation, the national president of the convention organization took the podium and began lambasting the newsroom dignitary for associating blindness and visual impairments with health issues. This national president went into an entire tirade, chastising that blindness and vision impairments are social issues rather than health problems. All this time, I kept thinking to myself, *[is the leader of this organization totally clueless to the severe headaches, fatigue, depression, and other health maladies related to vision loss?*

This organization's head honcho simply could not relate to or even understand the differences within his own constituency. His viewpoint saw vision loss as a totality rather than accepting its different dimensions. At times, he referred to residual eyesight as unreliable vision and seemed to criticize those of us who did not walk with white canes and read by braille. Even the use of a guide dog versus a white cane fostered scrutiny by this group. Instead of being inspirational, the biased commentary turned me away from their membership. It really felt like having and using any remaining acuity created resentment and accusations of denial by this group. A colleague of mine later described this organization as a bad religion, which preaches nothing but fire and brimstone, while condemning anyone who fails to abide by its sermons. These experiences reminded me of a line from the Beatle song "Nowhere Man," which sings, "He's as blind as he can be, just sees what he wants to see, nowhere man can you see me at all."

After returning back home to Oregon, my local chapter asked me to brief them about the convention. I did so without holding back any of the details. My concerns were reinforced by fellow members, who voiced likewise antagonisms. As the year ended, this local chapter voted to disband and donate their remaining treasury funds to Guide Dogs for the Blind. Upon learning of our actions, the state president somehow put a stop to our donation and had all local funds transferred to her state account. Disgusted by this vindictive action, the local members reorganized a new chapter with another national organization that proved to be a lot less controversial and more resourceful.

Until you fully enter the fray, most folks are unaware of the civil wars that exist between and within many advocacy groups. While vying for members and majority rule, each lays claim to knowing what is best for their constituents. As a result, the political actions of these organizations often nurture more division than unity. In doing so, they sadly alienate the sage leaders needed to guide them.

These unfortunate experiences really educated me as to why so many talented achievers shy away from getting involved with advocacy issues. The bad taste created by the militant and self-serving entities is hard to swallow. Having served on the boards of United Way, American Cancer Society, RSVP, and other reputable organizations, I know firsthand the immense value of these groups. Based on my personal encounters, I now shy away from those who primarily ruffle feathers, and instead, focus on the groups with not only the fortitude to keep all their ducks in a row, but also foster the wherewithal for even the ugliest ones to someday blossom into swans.

In Coldest Blood

When life becomes a slippery slope, just go with the snow.

This endeavor of mine was supposed to be cool, but then it got cold, really, really, cold, and sometimes more frigid yet. Before I knew it, my life suddenly entered too many treacherous paths and began rapidly heading down a slippery slope. Too numb to react, my descent continued further into the deep freeze. Even now, I still shudder uncontrollably when recalling what transpired. All of this, due to a dire hotshot quest for a legacy.

Life has its twists and turns, which can be greatly amplified by the choices one makes. During my college years, a rampant Scandinavian fever broke out in this neck of the woods. As snowfalls occurred, the lure of the Nordic ski drifted in. This frosty frenzy began recreationally and then got fiercely competitive. Needing additional physical education credits at my Wisconsin university, I signed on for the cross-country skiing class and soon became afflicted. Shortly after completing this course, I scrounged through my limited financial resources and collected enough to purchase a set of wooden skis, leather boots, and bamboo poles. I then headed for the winding trails, where everything got more complex and chaotic.

Once again, I found myself in a position of being scared silly. Rocketing downhill and through the woods on skinny skis is a thrill indeed. However, the view from the top can be incredibly harrowing when the runs, bumps, and turns ahead of you are somewhat out of sight. Such was my case. Guided by my peripheral acuity and extremely reactive reflexes, I managed to escape close encounters with the ice, snow, and immovable objects. At times, this also included other skiers. In fact, when it came to stops and maneuvers, I literally had to be better than most.

A major part of my college campus life included involvement with an outdoors organization dubbed "The Hobbits." Its members prided themselves in pursuing challenges such as whitewater rafting, kayaking, cave exploring, bike touring, backpacking, wilderness canoeing, camping, rock climbing, and hardcore hiking. As Nordic skiing gained popularity, the Hobbits made it their goal to test every trail within a day's drive. This translated into more glide-and-slide tours then ever imagined.

Among these hobbits was a guy named Ron. Festooned with golden whiskers, a Gortex parka, and Vasque hiking boots, Ron had the adventurous look of a model in an REI catalog. He also possessed elevated powers of persuasion that would entice you to run any river, ski any trail, trek any path, and bike any course. He even got many of us to spelunk into tight places and depths below. Ron's influence would now strike once again.

Just when it seemed that far too many challenges had already been met, Ron discovered a unique cross-country ski race being held in the Wisconsin north woods. It was called the American Birkebeiner and mimicked the legendary rescue of the Norwegian prince, when ski-clad Viking loyalists carried him to safety over a fifty-five kilometer sojourn. This royal infant later became King Haakon Haakonson IV. Norway annually holds its own replication of this 13th century odyssey, and now America had its own version as well. Convinced by Ron's gift of gab, I now found myself among a clan of Nordic neophytes and headed northbound. We had registered for this unconventional event without most of us having any real idea of what fifty-five kilometers represented or how difficult it would be to cover this distance during a mid-February Wisconsin winter. And except for me, no one else in the crowded vanload of Hobbits had any idea what an audacious challenge this presented to a particular passenger.

Being young and immortal has its advantages, but there are limits. Perhaps I should have recognized my own before embarking on this adventurous trek. With no pun intended, the ups and downs of this outrageous ordeal did not represent a level playing field for me. Nonetheless, this was a chance to prove my ability to go the distance and overcome barriers. Never mind that one previous but isolated incident when I failed to recognize a protruding branch on a downhill run and allowed it to snag my ski tip. I eventually recovered from the concussion and almost never experienced a tumble quite so discombobulating. Never mind the fact as well, that I had gotten off track during a prior ski race through unfamiliar territory. By somehow missing a strategic arrow sign, I ended up several kilometers off course. If not for a group of sympathetic rabbit hunters lending me directions, I would have been left guessing which logging road to go down next. And just for the record, I am not the first or last racer to wander off course and make a wrong turn. Nonetheless, with these experiences behind me, I was now Birkie bound.

Prior to the 9:00 a.m. start of this event, I gathered with other anxious racers in a huge prep room at the Telemark Lodge. Everyone around me was hastily applying concoctions to the bases of their skis. Many were speaking languages other than English. These foreigners came equipped with huge boxes of multicolored substances and completed their wax applications with flaming torches. One guy even accidentally backed into an active torch, which suddenly set the back side of his ski suit aflame. This poor soul then ran frantically out of the building and jumped hurriedly into an extinguishing snow bank.

Overwhelmed by the chemistry and calamity surrounding me, I timidly migrated to a corner of this waxing enclave and pulled out my slab of Jackrabbit dry snow wax. After rubbing this pine tar onto my skis, I corked it smooth and then added just a thin layer of Jackrabbit wet snow wax, for extra traction. No fancy formulas, flamethrowers, flat-irons, or scrapers were part of my technique.

When race time arrived and skiers began lining up on the course, I found myself among a thousand-plus hyped-up competitors. Many like me were rookie participants, layered in cable-knit sweaters, makeshift wool knickers, snowflake-patterned knee socks, long johns, and naive aspirations. A few native Cheeseheads even wore their toasty hunting hats and jackets. Looking around, it took only a few moments to become intimidated by the Lycra-skinned Europeans, some of whom were future or former Olympians and national team members. Perhaps a more judicious heed of these seasoned racers should have been taken into consideration. Nonetheless, I positioned myself near the front of the starting line. In years to come, there would be segregated waves based on proven performances, yet at this stage in the Birkie's history, even a nimrod like me could mingle among the mighty. Therefore, I was about to be engulfed in a mass start free-for-all.

As the cannon sounded and skiers simultaneously erupted forward, the entire scene turned into a jumble of flailing poles and crossed ski tips. Obscenities ensued as skis, poles, arms, and legs entangled within the melee. There were human pileups from the domino effect of colliding bodies. Even at the very start, it became evident that this race would become more a matter of survival than a mere competition. In the back of my mind, I kept recalling the quote made the evening before at the carbo-loading spaghetti feed. A veteran Norwegian racer named Sven Wik advised all his fellow competitors to "start out slow and taper off." It now made sense.

Engulfed in such malarkey, my impending burden involved racing a far greater distance than I had ever skied in one day. This showdown also entailed an unforgiving terrain that physically and mentally drains its challengers. The sojourn began with an ungracious trudge up a steep ski slope called "*Valhalla*". Although the term *Valhalla* refers to the nirvana of Norse mythology, ascending this contentious grade represented a hellish ordeal. The unrelenting climb required a leg-stretching herringbone all the way to the summit. Upon cresting the mini mountain, now facing me was a mind-boggling vertical drop down the backside. Never before had I dodged so many crashes on one hill. Skiers were somersaulting into snow banks and each other. Detached skis flew by me like hell-bound missiles. Those who made it to the bottom in one piece suddenly confronted an immense logjam of racers, as the trail narrowed into the woods.

Next to come on this course was a continuous rollercoaster ride known as the "Powerline." Farther along came a screaming downward plunge named "Bitch Hill." No margin for error existed on this bobsled-like run. From this point on, the race transpired into an ongoing physical and mental skirmish to make it from one food station to another. Finally as the finish drew near, a dismal winding route dragged on and on, as it crossed an icy lake. Added to all this, were the brutal winter conditions of the Wisconsin north woods. As racers periodically glided past me, just as many struggling competitors simply pulled off the course to recuperate. Over hill and dale, the Birkie quickly established whether you were a tortoise or a hare.

Based on my unique situation, I welcomed the multitudes. It was part of my strategy to proceed onward with skiers all around

me. No need to get sidetracked and lost this time. The small signposts indicating progress and whereabouts often got missed. It didn't really matter, because in this race you just set a pace and go with the flow until the next food station is reached. Located every seven to ten kilometers, these food stops continually became ongoing sanity checkpoints. While refueling, you often found yourself debating whether to trudge on or relinquish.

Along the rough and tumble route, I witnessed more than a few calamitous crashes. Broken poles and skis were not anomalies. Broken spirits were just as frequent among the competitors, who oftentimes, stepped off the course to recompose while assessing a continuation. Some skiers opted to compete in the Korteloppet race, a half-length Birkebeiner. Real men like me, however, must go the entire distance. I still remember reaching the midpoint of this journey and praying for divine intervention. In exchange for helping me to complete this unholy pilgrimage, I pledged never to do anything so crazy again.

After four and a half hours of slipping and sliding, my plea for mercy was about to succeed. With less than a kilometer of homestretch to go, the PA system belted out my name and residency. Being distinguished by this unexpected announcement, I gained a desperately needed shot of adrenalin. The last stage involved a jaunt through the streets of downtown Hayward. Cheering spectators seemed to be everywhere along this remaining distance. Adding to the fanfare, many shook loud clanging cowbells. With what little energy I still had remaining, my stride went into a mode of full speed ahead. Upon crossing the finish line, I then needed assistance to remain standing as the Birkebeiner medal got draped over my head. With a few tears of relief and joy, I cradled this medal of mettle and reflected on what had just been accomplished. Over hill and dale, you need not finish first to be a winner in this incredible race. Surviving is the real reward. For me, however, the Birkie proved my ability to prevail among some of the best athletes in the world. In this course of life and throughout the long run, I was now as good as anyone else.

At last, my diehard yearning to become a Road Runner character had finally succeeded. During the next two decades, I completed twenty consecutive Birkebeiners and got inducted into the Birchleggings Club. The term *Birchleggings* is derived from the Viking era, when birch bark shin wrappings served as gaiters for travel through deep snows.

In the third year of my Birkie pursuits, the course changed directions and finished at Telemark. This now meant a demoralizing climb up "Bitch Hill" during the second half of the race and surviving the "Powerline," as the finish drew near. This anxiety resulted in the race reverting once again back to a Telemark start, with a rerouting around "Valhalla." Two of my odysseys took place in polar single digit temperatures, which required a Vaseline facial for frostbite protection. Due to the severe sub-freezing conditions, those with heavily bewhiskered facades, often formed dripping icicles of perspiration along their numbed face lines. Huge bonfires were ignited as warming relief near the starting line. Skiers sometimes shrouded themselves with plastic garbage bags while awaiting the race start. Water bottles became useless because of frozen tops. Overmitts and facemasks saved many from frostbite.

Every year represented a different encounter. Fresh snow versus old snow created waxing anxieties. The coldest coverings caused an abrasive friction. When really butt-freezing frigid, the snow squeaked like Styrofoam being stepped on. Sometimes an icy glaze on the trails turned every hill into panic mode. At the opposite extreme, meltdowns often warmed the snow to a consistency of instant mashed potatoes, dismally causing your skis to slog miserably through the off-white muck.

The formative years of the Birkie were quite different than nowadays. You never knew what to expect, such as the two racers who skied tandem on one pair of skis or the poor soul who finished the race using a tree branch to replace his two broken poles. The hand-drumming duo just before the midway point added fanfare. Somewhere amidst the second half of the race, a gang with the look of bikers, gathered alongside the trail. On their right hung an Old Glory unfurled. Just to the left of them blared a boom box with Steppenwolf tunes of "Born to be Wild" and "Magic Carpet Ride." Centered in the middle of this cheering clan sat a tapped keg. As the music interjected energy into your stride, the beer tempted you to linger.

The food stations themselves differed somewhat in these times. The energy drink was a liquid concoction that smelled like dill pickle juice. Wholesome donut holes served as one of the fuel supplements. The more nutritious orange slices became a hindrance and hazard. Because the majority of racers still relied on gooey klistered bases, the castoff orange peels readily stuck to the ski bottoms. As emergency rations, you could rely on the Nature Valley granola bars and Whoppers candies found in your race packet.

Just beyond these food stops were wax stations, where, upon request, you were tossed any kick wax of your choice. By making a brief stay at each of these Swix distribution points, you could finish the race with enough waxes for next season and beyond.

My favorite Birkie remains to be the year a group of anxious competitors, jumpstarted the race, almost fifteen minutes early. Instead of waiting for the cannon to signal the start, some of the European racers mistook the PA announcement and bolted off in full stride. In response, those of us also at the starting gates simply followed. Meanwhile, skiers who had not yet fastened on their skis scrambled madly to dash onto the course and join the melee. In the midst of this scramble, a news media helicopter descended for a close-up filming of the chaos. In doing so, the whirlybird dropped so low that its' rotating blades stirred the powdery course surface into a full blown blizzard.

Also worthy of recollection is the year of the incredible pileup. While I waited for my second wave to begin five minutes later, the front wave of speed demons shot forward. As they approached the sloping first turn on the trail, a mass entanglement ensued. One skier after another collided into a stockpile of competitors. By the time they completely unraveled, my wave began arriving on the scene.

Following my second Birkie, the cherished wooden Janoy skis and bamboo poles got set aside in favor of Rossignol fiberglass racing skis and Swix carbon-tipped poles. Those toe-contorting three-pin bindings gave way to Nordic Norm upgrades. Both my klister waxes and hodgepodge outfits changed over to a slicker format of fluorocarbons and Lycra. At one point, even my techniques switched. I tried twice to complete the Birkie as a fast-paced skater, but eventually reverted back to my methodical classic striding. Only once did I break a ski and injure a body part. Along with this, there were several minor hit-and-runs. Through it all, I always managed to finish in the middle of the pack, which often swelled to well over six thousand racers. To accommodate the hordes, the trail got widened into a skiers' freeway. Sophisticated grooming reduced the bumps and softened the icy spots. The entire trail became fine-tuned with grooved tracks for the classic striders and smooth surfaces for the accelerating skaters.

On the steep and curving downhill runs of the Birkie course, I had to proceed with more caution than most racers. My snowplowing at a reduced pace really irked any speedsters overtaking me on these descents. At times, I ended up either sideswiped or cursed. In one particular encounter, I even got completely run over. My response to these cussing tailgaters was always the same, "If you are so damn fast, why aren't you already ahead of me?"

Throughout this same era, I also competed internationally in the Worldloppet ski marathons of Austria, Germany, Italy, Sweden, and Canada. The longest of these races was the seventy kilometer (forty-two miles) Marcialonga, which crossed through fourteen Italian villages. During this more than six hour Italian ordeal on skinny skis, the villagers often shouted, "Bravo, Yankee" after seeing the American flag patch on my ski uniform. I could never figure out whether I was being cheered as a visiting competitor or sarcastically commended for trailing behind their homegrown racers.

The sixty-five kilometer Konig Ludwig Lauf of Germany ventured past castles and old ruins. The sixty kilometer Austrian race cascaded through the alpine Dolomites. Had it not been significantly shortened because of weather conditions, the Swedish Vasaloppet would have measured ninety kilometers. The toughest of these marathons, however, was the fifty-five kilometer Quebec Gatineau Loppet, where it had rained the day before and then turned to treacherous ice over night. My body still recalls the haphazard face-plants throughout this horrific race. On one hill alone, I crashed three times. At one point on this dangerous course, skiers were actually sliding off a hairpin curve and landing in a flowing creek. Several of these Worldloppet races have now been reduced in length.

Here in the states, there were other adventures as well, which included racing along the rim of Southern Oregon's Crater Lake, joining the Great Ski Race from Lake Tahoe to Truckee, zigzagging down a trail named Psycho from the timberline ridges at Donner Pass, viewing Lake Tahoe from Diamond Peak, scaling Echo Summit and retracing the legendary Sierra treks of Snowshoe Thompson, striding the Vasaloppet course over the frozen fields of Northern Minnesota, back country tripping into the Wallow Range, dodging odorous steam spouts in Northern California's Lassen Volcanic Park, climbing atop Colorado's Crested Butte, scurrying around Mount Bachelor in central Oregon, enduring subzero odysseys among moose herds along the Gunflint Trail and Boundary Waters near Canada, groping through a whiteout in the Blue Mountains of Washington, and jaunts around the cascading loops of Northern Wisconsin's Underdown and Eagle River trail systems. .

Hopelessly addicted to this sport, Nordic skiing had become a major part of my life. Although my full-time work resulted in moves around the country, I would only consider positions with a close proximity to snow country. By doing so, I became an established Nordic instructor at ski centers in California, Nevada, Oregon, Wisconsin, and Minnesota. Freelancing as a seasonal ski reporter, I also became a regular contributor to the *Sierra Outdoors, Tahoe Times, Birch Scroll*, and several other winter sports publications. During a six-year stint at the Tahoe Donner Nordic Center, my teaching role became specialized in adaptive skiing. Because of a Sacramento snow angel named Betsy, I assisted the Sierra Regional Ski for Light program and also served as a lead instructor for the National Disabled Veterans Winter Sports Festival in Colorado.

Oftentimes my instruction involved students whom others had given up on. I still recall my proudest moment teaching a young man named George, who was deaf, legally blind, and cognitively impaired. Through the assistance of his interpreter, my instructions to George were drawn in his hand as the primary form of communication. When we completed the ski loop that day, I 'm not sure who was more excited, George or me. My students often taught me lessons as well. While teaching with the Winter Special Olympics, I was assigned to Steven, a student with a major speech impediment and learning disorder. Throughout the training, I marveled at the way Steven precisely followed my demonstrations on the trail. As the day ended, I was asked about this student's progress by the program coordinator. After praising Steven's athleticism and balance, I then noted a personal frustration with the lack of his response to my cheers and verbal feedback. When told that he was deaf, I felt like an idiot for failing to pick up on this. Then again, my own encounters often placed me in a similar situation. It is amazing how we sometimes expect those with hearing or vision limitation to have a certain look about them.

Based on my personal experiences and those of others I have met, challenging adversity often results in elevated scrutiny. While living in Bend, Oregon, I learned of a local teenage girl named Rachael, whose goal was to participate in the legendary Iditarod, Alaska's one thousand mile dogsled race. Because of faulty headlights similar to mine, this feisty gal's aspirations were often criticized as ridiculous and unrealistic. However, Rachael prevailed in this lifetime dream. I also became acquainted with a triathlon competitor from California, who race organizers attempted to bar because of his limited visual acuity. They considered him an accident just waiting to happen, but failed to also consider that he was married to an attorney with a heightened awareness of the ADA. The last I heard, this guy is again training and competing. While working at Tahoe Donner, I marveled at the two paraplegic skiers who trained here and succeeded in sit-skiing unassisted over the Sierras.

During my early years of ski races and excursions, I often feared being excluded should the limited extent of my acuity be fully realized. It is an unfortunate reality that stereotyping and prejudice causes far too many to fixate on what you cannot do, rather than what you can. Sometimes viewed as a liability, there were instances when ski centers and students shied away from me as an instructor. Whenever this happened, I then waxed up and headed solo into the hills. Being out and about on any course was, of course, just fine with me.

Sour Grapes of Wrath

Sour grapes and a little wrath, make for a fine whine.

Sometimes life becomes a dimmer switch. Slowly but surely the lights are being turned down. Occurring ever so slightly, this predicament seems almost unnoticeable. Eventually the evidence becomes all too clear, which then really clouds things up. What now confronts you is by no means a circumstance for sissies.

During my federal government career, life's challenges started catching up with me. I reluctantly began noticing what I no longer noticed. Seeing the world around me was becoming more difficult. Headaches and other maladies surfaced frequently while straining to make it through each workday. Both the small print and headlines faded gradually away, while everyday recognition of those around me caused far too many awkward moments. Without giving up or giving in, I tried all kinds of adaptations, but never could my eyes simply shut down and be prevented from working overtime. As such, the reality of all this, led to early federal retirement, which created a well-needed physical respite, which got countered by a fair amount of guilty uneasiness.

In the years that followed my exit from full-time employment, complete departure from the workplace had to be amended. After moving to Oregon and earning certification as a mediator, I soon found myself enlisted part-time at a dispute resolution center. Thanks again to help from the DVR folks, this new office of mine got outfitted with a fully-adapted computer system. My background in being the complaints department for the feds really benefited me in this realm. Involved with dozens of cases, another niche had been established. This endeavor also tapped my journalism background by enticing me to pen monthly advice columns titled *"Mending Fences* and *Business Resolve."* The limited hours of this job allowed me to avoid some of the difficulties previously encountered on a full-time basis. However, something happened to me that is not all that unusual. I became seriously homesick for my home state of Wisconsin. My parents were aging, and the cross-country phone calls were not enough of a connection. When my mother got admitted for quadruple heart bypass surgery, assessing the situation from long distance was not enough. Not only did I feel compelled to return back home, but I also really wanted my daughter, Brianna, to become better acquainted with her grandparents, aunts, uncles, and cousins. What I really missed as well were my old trout fishing holes and the chance to tutor my brothers in angling pursuits.

While researching the help-wanted ads from my old stomping grounds, lo and behold, the same job I long ago held at a small University of Wisconsin college was once again open. Concurring with this omen, I applied and soon found myself Badger state bound for a familiar role as an advisor and student life coordinator. As such, this part-time position entailed coordinating campus clubs and events, advising student government and leadership programs, organizing orientations, and participating on various committees. Like my last job in Oregon, its limited hours appeared to accommodate my unusual situation.

Although the next five years involved achievements, a familiar nemesis continued to stalk me. I had flourished in this job by expanding and creating collegiate programs that ranged from sports to theater. My folk-singer past even got resurrected with routine performances at a campus venue called the Acoustic Café. Re-ignited as well were my writing passions through publication of short stories in the college's literary journal. Despite my successes, however, time was again taking its toll. The dimmer switch had continued to silently turn and make life more difficult. These faulty headlights of mine struggled to shine. Simultaneously, another kind of gloom began lurking.

Even though this university role was a part-time position with variable hours, my shifts were resurrecting chronic headaches, fatigue, and associated issues. Severe migraines routinely surfaced. Eyestrain transpired into excruciating neck pain, which, in turn, flared up backaches. The remedies themselves were also back-lashing with problems. Depression and anxiety crept in as well. With my headlights faltering more than ever, this overcast struggle phased into darker moments.

What became most difficult of all were the responses all around me. Becoming less able to recognize and greet my colleagues led to complaints of me being unfriendly or snobbish. Some even considered me sinister or distrustful due to my lack of direct eye contact. Relying almost entirely on peripheral acuity, I evolved into the campus sidewinder through descriptions of being shifty eyed, cockeyed, and lazy eyed. A reoccurring put down referenced me as "a guy who just won't look you straight in the eye." Even though I felt that I was peering directly at individuals, there were increasing occasions of being chastised for not paying attention. Unable to literally see eye to eye, my visual cues led to ongoing misconceptions. Those who tried reading my eyes could not understand the blank pages they were presently viewing and attempting to decipher.

The workplace environment became so antagonizing that I finally resorted to sending out an e-mail to faculty, staff, and student leaders. In my message, I explained about my faulty headlights and some of the difficulties currently being experienced. This became my version, so to speak, of coming out of the closet. By doing so, I faced the risk of becoming the campus Mr. Magoo. Instead, this got me perceived as a conniving Wily Coyote interfering with the Road Runner progress of this college. Although the feedback included commendations of courage, skepticism burgeoned as well. Some of those with the highest levels of education felt they knew better and thus bolstered the most scrutiny of my sounding off. What probably hurt the most at this pillar of higher education however, were the responses from my boss.

Some folks just don't get it. My boss seemed to be one of them. While confidentially advised with the medical details, this supervisor never really grasped the severity of my ongoing acuity loss. Perhaps I was partly to blame. Fearful of both prejudice and embarrassment, I was not always comfortable disclosing all the health- and work-related issues to this guy. However, I oftentimes had no choice but to confide in a boss, whose past meetings frequently interjected disparaging religious perspectives and a disbelief of my dilemma. In one instance, he even professed the claim that I was exaggerating my disability status to gain some kind of advantage. In the same biased manner, which some refer to as "playing the race card," his accusation implied the laying down of a disability card. This reference represented one of the most disgusting allegations I have ever encountered. In rebuttal, I stood up and left his office. Feeling betrayed, I wasn't sure if I could ever trust or respect this man again. Even though all of us harbor prejudices, those held by some are not always kept under control. When any bias suddenly breaks loose, the ugliness is indelibly unleashed.

During my time at this public institution, prior tensions had grown between my boss and me. Much of this stemmed from his religious convictions. He boasted of being a bishop within a church well-known for its proselytizing, something I now routinely experienced and rejected. Feeling targeted for conversion, I dreaded conversations with this high-ranking member of the administration. All too often, I ended up waiting outside his office, while he conducted church business over the phone. Initially afraid to voice concerns, I was intimidated by this right-hand man and close friend of the campus dean.

The faith to which my boss belonged had a controversial

history, which included harems, baptism by proxy, blood-atonement ceremonies, and biases toward women, minorities, sexual orientations, and other faiths. Also discovered about this following was a strange proclamation that loyal congregation males are prophetically granted their own planets with ladies in waiting. During my mediation career, a revealing case came before me, through which I became exposed to this sect's dark ages. One of this church's earliest leaders actually professed that people of color had been created to represent the devil. Another aspect of its theology was that Native Americans were not an indigenous people, but rather nomadic Israelites. The Jewish Holocaust database maintained by this group to baptize these victims into another faith is totally bizarre. As for the sacred undergarment ritual, this eccentric practice is all too strange. As absurd as all of this may sound, it is a matter of record confirmed by many religious scholars.

Previously, I had been offered a job in the city, where this denomination is headquartered. After delving into some extensive research, the discoveries were mind-boggling. Quite frankly, they scared the bajeebers out of me. Even PBS produced an alarming documentary about the history of this faith. Three different clergy members I confided in, at times, used the term *"cult"* to describe this congregation. Obviously, I rejected the job offer and eventually ended up confronting the dilemma of being supervised and judged by a leader within this following. Guilty of my own beliefs, I held my own bias against the foundations of my boss's affiliation.

An engrained past experience caused me to be jaded in this circumstance. During my time in the federal government, a mind-boggling discovery threw me off-kilter. A very popular and respected colleague, one day made reference to KKK ties. When I mentioned this commentary to another colleague, she concurred of hearing the same, but wanted no further discussion on this topic. In what seemed like campus déjà vu,

I once again had to deal with another influential individual, whose morals collided with mine.

From several conversations with my boss, his religious convictions became quite evident. One of the issues which caught my attention involved his judging of sexual orientation. What really seemed ironic to me was that any gay student on this campus facing animosity got directed to an administrator, who boldly led a church which adamantly condemned the gay community. Oftentimes I wondered how this scenario would have affected someone like my college friend John. Perhaps this dynamic even impacted the short-term stay of a gay Sri Lankan professor at this campus. Whether it did or not, this peculiarity undermined sensitivity and inclusion.

If my accounts sound overcritical toward this supervisor's particular affiliation, it is just that I do not condone religious groups who arrogantly attempt to impose their beliefs on others, while disregarding certain aspects of their faith's heritage. Most of all, there is nothing sacred about practices, past or present, which discriminate on the basis of race, religion, gender, or otherwise. Although I was raised Catholic, I am equally critical of this denomination's opposition to women as priests and marriage for clergy. The Catholic Church's role in the Crusades and papal indulgences certainly reflects a questionable history. And please, do not get me started on the altar boy issues which some grade school buddies of mine sadly experienced.

One of my most disappointing encounters on this campus involved an issue brought to me by a Jewish student. Allegedly, a faculty member shouted out a warning for others to stay away from this student or risk being circumcised. It had been my own experience to hear this same professor refer to a specific racial group as the enemy, label those with German heritage as Nazis, and I will not repeat what he supposedly called one of the Middle Eastern professors. My position required that I notify administration of any such conduct. What I then encountered was a "kill the messenger" rebuttal. This made me gun-shy of disclosing reports of inappropriate remarks directed toward me as well.

Another friction created between my supervisor and I involved a nontraditional student named Cyrus. Because of his age, this senior citizen was entitled to non-credit enrollment in college classes. As a disability, his mental health status also entitled him to audit these classes. In doing so, Cyrus was far from your ordinary higher education participant. I got to know him through various campus events. He regularly attended poetry readings and played a founding role in creating the college's literary journal. Distinguished with neatly groomed silvery whiskers and dapper hats, this character bore a slight resemblance to Earnest Hemingway. His literary background further added to this comparison.

Cyrus was both a talented writer and former English educator. Unfortunately, the circumstances of a medical condition estranged him from his career and lifestyle. As a result, Cyrus now lived alone in a downtown motel room and had no personal means of transportation. With the university nearby, he maintained access to education, something he so dearly cherished. In conversations with Cyrus, he hinted to me about both Vietnam and schizophrenia, but would never elaborate on either.

Cyrus represented an invaluable opportunity for students and faculty members to interact with someone from an intriguing walk of life. Some, however, just did not see it that way. Uncomfortable with his intermittent ranting and quirky behavior, Cyrus got booted from this campus. Although I am not aware of all the circumstances, I saw the exodus of Cyrus as a lack of advocacy and understanding. Similar to my friend Frank, this loner at times made others uncomfortable. And yet, like Frank, Cyrus was an incredibly talented individual. Minus his presence, the campus seemed somewhat empty. With the loss of Cyrus, this place forfeited its ability to advocate, intervene, and compromise. What he desired so deeply was to intellectually fit in, but ironically, it became those perceived as esteemed intellectuals, who ultimately dashed this challenged man's modest hopes and dreams.

Intended or not, the mandated departure of Cyrus echoed a message that persons with disabilities were not always welcome on this campus. It made you pause and wonder as to whether others with physical or mental challenges would receive the same scrutiny. By no means an isolated event, this Cyrus episode certainly made someone in my situation feel threatened by what appeared to be a hostile environment. As my faulty headlights flickered, would I be dubbed the next weirdo to go? Matched up against other campuses I had experienced, this UW two year college paled in comparison when it came to disability services and understanding.

Adding to this concern, I got lambasted one day while discussing policies at a multicultural committee meeting. Seated across the table from me was an outspoken professor well known for his expletives and controversial conduct. When I disagreed with a statement made by this educator, he jumped up, leaned forward, and screamed, "Are you f___ing blind?" A bonehead remark that equates blindness to stupidity should never be made to any individual, especially someone with faulty headlights. Perhaps oversensitive, this personal affront bugged me for days. Upon later discussing the incident with a campus administrator, she retorted that the conduct of this particular professor was simply his customary style of communicating. Her advice was to ignore it. Unfortunately, Cyrus was never afforded the same excuse and advisory. The general disregard for sensitivity at this campus kept eating at me. My past experiences on federal EEO and state ADA committees tugged at me to take an advocacy stand. The straws had accumulated, and this camel's back of mine, now seemed destined to break quite soon.

As my diminishing acuity caused escalating physical difficulties, it took a mental toll as well. Like never before in my lifetime, I had reached a critical crossroads. My ophthalmologist rated my central vision at less than 20/400. That huge "E" on the eye chart was now becoming just a mere memory. Even though previously unable to get through to my boss, I needed to bring forth updated accommodation needs. In the back of my mind, I still recollected this supervisor's previous diatribe about me trying to exploit my disability for an advantage.

When requiring upgraded accommodations, this stage can be incredibly intimidating. While not wanting to be viewed as a problem, you now represent needs which can result in tedious and pricey adaptations. Furthermore, there is never a guarantee that these remedies will work or defray further requirements. Your value as an asset now tips more toward liability. For this reason, coming forward with all the details is no easy task.

To be honest, my out of sight status caused problems beyond work as well. During a family photo session, the photographer almost went into rage mode while trying to get me to look straight at the camera. I thought I was doing so, but apparently not. In comical contrast, I still recall the city bus driver requesting me to move further back so that a boarding blind person could take my up-front seat. When handed an electronic game at a dinner party and asked to read the trivia question, the entire room succumbed to an eerie silence when I noted that I just could not see it. This triggered a third grade flashback. More than once, I have been called a bum for making my wife pump the gas into our van. Telling such bozos that I cannot adequately see the gas meter would have been futile. Every day generated varying conundrums. However, when these experiences become consistently negative in the workplace, my ADA training taught me to seek resolutions.

While explaining this situation one day to my boss, he interrupted by comparing my disability status to his religious affiliation. He then proceeded with a lengthy sermon about the misunderstood merits of his denomination and how some family members have estranged him for his beliefs. I wanted to debate that my fading acuity was not a choice like that of his religion. However, it was now being made quite clear to me that he continued lacking the wherewithal to fully understand my predicament.

There finally came a day when my direct supervisor's unwelcome commentaries and the events around me reached an intolerable threshold. Fed up and unable to ignore it any longer, I filed a formal complaint. Aware of the potential consequences, this was not something that I relished doing. As an initial result, a supervisory change got assigned for several months. However, when I naively agreed for my former boss to later again be my direct supervisor, the payback began. My hours were slashed and activities curtailed. Just when the student government, which I advised, was about to receive the statewide Chancellor's Award for Excellence, my boss peppered me with a bevy of accusations about mismanaging this organization. I then countered with a complaint of retaliation, and the payback turned uglier.

The stigma now bestowed on me was that of a black sheep undergoing constant fleecing. Prior to this unrelenting scrutiny, my evaluations had been stellar. However, everything suddenly went sour after raising concerns and requiring further accommodations. Even the confidential complaint I had filed, met with retaliation from others. Ambushed at a multicultural committee meeting, two professors brazenly violated protection rights and openly attacked my complaint. Their vindictive rhetoric took place in front of a room full of students. Not only was I humiliated by this hostile action, but also totally disgusted by the lesson they were teaching to the students on this campus.

Challenging the old guard meant the welcome mat no longer existed. This time there was no Bill to help adapt or Lester providing protection. Realizing that my contract was about to expire, a tough decision had to be made. With duties and hours in disarray, I decided to salvage my well-being and end this five year stint. I understood from the beginning, that busting through barriers doesn't always result in happy endings. Ignoring the events around me, did not serve as an option. My rebuttals had rocked the boat at this institution. And to be quite honest, I can make no claim to being an angel throughout this process.

In fairness to this boss of mine, he confronted major personal struggles. Diagnosed with cancer, his health and disposition faced serious challenges. Regardless of religious convictions, this bewildering disease brought with it the usual fears, anger, and uncertainty. Like Lester's bout with cancer, there were irritable and irrational episodes. My boss definitely had to be hurting more so than me. With so much on his plate, perhaps dealing with my trials and tribulations, simply could not be empathized with at this juncture.

As a gun-slinging "reactivist," I usually shoot back when the bullets came flying my way. Although misfiring a few times, many of my potshots have hit the mark and been right on target. This does not necessarily make me the good guy in a white hat. ADA and EEO disputes seem to turn everyone involved into rivaling outlaws. Settling such disagreements unfortunately culminate into far too many battle cries and war injuries.

Now drawn into a bitter campus skirmish, more than a fair share of this contest had already been fought. This process would eventually run its course, letting the cards fall where they may. Within this state institution, the investigation of my complaint and its ADA/EEO implications opened up a huge can of worms. It triggered system-wide issues. The chancellor, general counsel, and other state officials became involved. From what I heard, a certain professor got reprimanded. Apparently, this fiasco also took its toll on the local dean of students and the state human resources director, both of whom suddenly stepped down from their lofty positions following the outcome. Of course, this may have been nothing but an uncanny coincidence. All this crossfire made me a casualty as well.

Because of my hypersensitivity to adversity, the battles I fought were often those of others, as well as mine. Each skirmish reminded me of my dorm mate Fred, my fix-it friend Michael, my writer colleague Cyrus, my strumming buddy Frank, and the many disabled vets I had met. Although we cannot all be activists, within every one of us needs to be an advocate.

The reason why Equal Employment Opportunity (EEO) and Americans with Disabilities Act (ADA) exist lies in the fact that discrimination is an unfortunate reality. Filing a complaint however, enters you into a contest that is far from fair. The reaction can turn into retaliation rather than resolution. Regardless of your right to bring forth concerns, doing so pits you against a system that uses everything in its power to fight back and often characterize the complainant as the culprit. My personal experiences in this arena range from hellish interrogations to "fist in the face" threats. This realm is certainly not one for sissies.

At this stage in my life, neither the university job nor the hostility was needed. Besides, I had better things to do. With my acuity diminishing and perseverance waning, it was time to truly retire once and for all. Behind me were successes in five different career fields. Perhaps now, with some DVR help again, I will experience a sixth by becoming an author of several books. Despite stomping the sour grapes of wrath related to my faulty headlights, this longtime literary goal is finally being accomplished. Quite possibly this means that retirement is still simmering on the backburner.

Over the years, I have grumbled far too much about God needing better quality control. Regardless of the fact that none of us comes with a warranty, there sure seems to be room for improvement on assembly and reliability. Having put more than enough miles on this chassis, I really should not complain. Aside from that major repair of six fuel lines, this motor still churns with a fair amount of horsepower. Currently under control, never mind the excess sugar recently discovered in the gas tank. Be assured, I am getting regular oil checks to keep on idling. As for that recent mechanical breakdown, it got taken care of by the same body shop, which, last year, removed my catalytic converter. Unable to be completely humble, the paint job and upholstery are still looking great. The tires seem pretty good as well. In many ways, I consider myself a restored classic. And although my headlights are stuck on the low beams and fading, this jalopy is in darn good running condition. Maybe it could even rumble and tumble through another Birkie. Then again, in the process of revealing all the chapters of this owner's manual, more than a few fenders have been sideswiped, bumpers dented, and lug nuts loosened. Therefore, prior to any more road trips, I might just need to spend the time reinforcing and armor-plating my rig.

Stated from the very beginning, I wanted to share the smirks, quirks, and irks of my unique endeavors. As a reality check, these perspectives are nothing more than a little light being cast by faulty headlights. Though wishing they were brighter, you shine the beams which life grants you. Considering all the potholes and rough roads that have been survived, I ought to be more thankful than cantankerous and overcritical. Perhaps after shifting gears, testing the brakes, and monitoring the dashboard indicators, the real message here has nothing to do with the model each of us drives, but rather how it is driven. And to do so, no license is required.

⌘⌘⌘⌘⌘⌘⌘⌘⌘⌘⌘⌘⌘⌘⌘⌘⌘⌘⌘⌘⌘⌘⌘⌘⌘⌘
⌘⌘⌘⌘⌘⌘⌘⌘⌘⌘⌘⌘⌘⌘⌘⌘⌘⌘⌘⌘⌘⌘⌘⌘⌘⌘

More tattles about the author & these stories are available from the website and e-mail address below:

folktattler.com or celticdan@frontier.com

⌘⌘⌘⌘⌘⌘⌘⌘⌘⌘⌘⌘⌘⌘⌘⌘⌘⌘⌘⌘⌘⌘⌘⌘⌘⌘
⌘⌘⌘⌘⌘⌘⌘⌘⌘⌘⌘⌘⌘⌘⌘⌘⌘⌘⌘⌘⌘⌘⌘⌘⌘⌘